A New Brooklyn Museum

Great edifices, like great mountains, are the work of ages.
—Victor Hugo

A New Brooklyn Museum
The Master Plan Competition

Edited by
Joan Darragh

Foreword by
Robert T. Buck

Introduction by
Reyner Banham

The Brooklyn Museum
and
Rizzoli, New York

Published for the exhibition
A NEW BROOKLYN MUSEUM: THE MASTER PLAN COMPETITION
March 11–July 4, 1988

The Brooklyn Museum Master Plan has been made possible by a
generous grant from the Sherman Fairchild Foundation. Additional
funds for the competition, exhibition, and publication have been
provided by the National Endowment for the Arts, the New York State
Council on the Arts, Joseph E. Seagram & Sons, Inc., and the Real
Estate Council of The Brooklyn Museum, under the chairmanship of
Arthur G. Cohen.

Project Director: Joan Darragh
Coordinator: Bailey Van Hook
Managing Editor: Elaine Koss
Editor: John Antonides

First published in the United States of America in 1988 by
Rizzoli International Publications, Inc.
597 Fifth Avenue, New York, New York 10017

Library of Congress Cataloging-in-Publication Data

Darragh, Joan.
   A New Brooklyn Museum.

   1. Brooklyn Museum.   2. Art museums—New York
(N.Y.)—Designs and plans.   3. Architecture—New York
(N.Y.)—Competitions.   4. Arata Isozaki & Associates—
Awards.   5. James Stewart Polshek and Partners—
Awards.   I. Brooklyn Museum.   II. Title.
N620.B6D37   1988   727′.7′0974723   87-42679
ISBN 0-8478-0863-7 (pbk.)

Cover:
Arata Isozaki & Associates/James Stewart Polshek and Partners
The Brooklyn Museum Master Plan Competition, north-south
longitudinal section, 1986.
Pages 4–5:
The Brooklyn Museum, Eastern Parkway (north) facade (photograph
by Patricia Layman Bazelon), 1985.
Page 6:
The Brooklyn Museum, aerial view looking northwest toward
Manhattan, 1985.

Design: Franchini + Cabana, Inc., New York City
Typesetting: David E. Seham Associates, Metuchen, New Jersey
Printing and binding: Dai Nippon Printing Co., Japan

Contents

A New Brooklyn Museum
The Master Plan Competition

Preface

A dictum followed by The Brooklyn Museum's founders in 1893 when they sponsored an architectural competition to determine a design for a museum building still holds true today: the facilities that house great public art collections should be glorious symbols of civic pride. In considering how to expand the building that resulted from that competition in order to accommodate the growth in the Museum's collections experienced during the twentieth century, the Museum's Board of Trustees wanted to rekindle the spirit of that age. To this end, on March 4, 1986, the Board held a special session at which it elected to sponsor an international invitational competition to produce a master plan to guide the Museum's reorganization and growth into the next century. As Chairman I am pleased to announce the winner of the competition—Arata Isozaki & Associates/James Stewart Polshek and Partners.

The competition process was extremely informative and the task of selecting one of the five skillful solutions a difficult challenge. I would like to express my deepest appreciation to the members of both the Selection Committee and the Jury, who met this challenge with continued enthusiasm, wisdom, and effort. A most-deserved special thanks goes to Director Robert T. Buck, who fostered the endeavor with leadership and confidence.

Alastair B. Martin
Chairman, Board of Trustees
The Brooklyn Museum

Foreword

Since 1934, The Brooklyn Museum building has undergone several interior and exterior renovations, the results of which have been—to our late twentieth-century sensibility—all too reductive and inconsistent with the original 1893 Beaux-Arts design. Approaching the centennial celebration in 1995 of the laying of the cornerstone of the McKim, Mead & White building, the Museum is faced with the responsibility of proposing and implementing a substantial capital improvement plan for its existing operating facilities and for developing programs that will respond to the institution's needs over the next century. During the 1980s, the Borough of Brooklyn, to which the fortunes of The Brooklyn Museum in great measure are bound, has been experiencing an important economic revival. Accordingly, the Museum has developed a plan that recognizes this development and provides for an ever more promising future.

In 1983, at the beginning of my term as Director, the Museum's capital plan consisted of little more than a list of needs left over from previous plans. Even though the rationale for their origin had become diluted by time, their longevity on the record confirmed their validity. One of the legacies from earlier times, for example, was the need for a new auditorium, which had been talked about since 1934, when the present lobby replaced the old auditorium. At the top of the list was a proper climate-control system, involving both air conditioning and humidity control, needs to which studies have attested during the past twenty years.

In general, the Museum's operational difficulties cluster around three resounding themes: the insufficiency of exhibition space, the absence of adequate art storage, and the dearth of public amenities. These difficulties are complicated by the building's incomplete and irregular state. The extant structure, whose facade historically typifies the nineteenth-century art museum, is somehow disturbingly akin to a Hollywood set. Behind the facade, an impossible circulation system confuses rather than engages the visitor. Simply put, as an art museum, the building doesn't function well enough.

14

As the institution has continued to develop and its spatial requirements have changed, the need for additional and improved space has become more and more crucial. Focusing on the growth in the Museum's holdings and bearing in mind the institution's programmatic needs, the Museum staff and consultants developed a long-term building program in preparation for the Master Plan Competition of 1986. For the second time in less than a century, architecture is guiding the course of The Brooklyn Museum. What began in 1893 with the firm of McKim, Mead & White will begin anew with the Arata Isozaki and James Stewart Polshek partnership.

The Brooklyn Museum Master Plan Competition has been the work of many people. Without the wisdom and support of Board Chairman Alastair B. Martin and encouragement from the Trustees—especially John A. Friede, Jeffrey C. Keil, Robert S. Rubin, and Mrs. Carl Selden, who tirelessly served on the Selection Committee and the Jury—there would have been no new beginning. My special thanks to Jeffrey C. Keil for his initial support of the idea to select an architect by competition and for his generosity in working so closely with and guiding the staff throughout the process. I am also grateful to our City partners on the Selection Committee—Ronay Menschel, representing Mayor Edward I. Koch, Linda Adams, representing Borough President Howard Golden, and Thomas Mangan, representing Commissioner of Cultural Affairs Bess Myerson. To the architects who served on the Jury, Klaus Herdeg, Phyllis Lambert, and James Stirling, and to Reyner Banham, who served on the Selection Committee, goes my deepest appreciation for sharing with us the considerable responsibility of selecting the architect and for adding their comforting and always illuminating professional expertise and wisdom. In addition, my thanks go to Linda S. Ferber, Chief Curator, who represented the staff so ably throughout.

The task of coordinating such an all-encompassing project as this could not have been in better hands than those of the capable and indefatigable Joan Darragh, Vice Director for Planning, who as project director for the competition, catalogue, and exhibition, has worked endless hours to ensure its success. I would also like to thank Terrance R. Williams, our Professional Advisor, whose enthusiasm and hard work helped set a model for the future. Thomas Krens, Director of the Williams College Museum of Art, deserves special thanks for helping us identify early on our management strengths and weaknesses.

I would like to add my congratulations and gratitude to the five finalists whose monumental efforts in devising solutions for the institution's problems have resulted in superb displays of the highest professional achievement, a testament to their dedication to the cause shared by us all. I can only say that clearly there was only one true winner of this competition: The Brooklyn Museum.

I am indebted to the Sherman Fairchild Foundation for its major support of our planning efforts. In addition, Joseph E. Seagram & Sons, Inc., and the Museum's newly formed Real Estate Council, headed by Arthur G. Cohen, contributed funds for the exhibition and publication. Lastly I wish to express my gratitude to the National Endowment for the Arts and to the New York State Council on the Arts for grants supporting, in part, the competition, publication, and exhibition and for their continued commitment to The Brooklyn Museum.

Robert T. Buck
Director
The Brooklyn Museum

Acknowledgments

This publication documents The Brooklyn Museum Master Plan Competition of 1986 and sets it within the historical framework of the institution. I am indebted to Reyner Banham and Leland Roth for their scholarship, criticism, and professionalism in placing the project within the proper critical and historical context.

My gratitude is further extended to the five finalists. It was an unforgettable experience and a privilege to have worked so closely with them and their design teams. I would like to express my deepest appreciation for their professional efforts as well as their dedication, spirit, stamina, and good humor. My thanks also to Professional Advisor Terrance R. Williams for overseeing the competition and developing the guidelines, program, and base documents, and to his associate Kevin Perry and the staff at Williams + Garretson for their diligence and camaraderie. I also want to thank Klaus Herdeg for his exacting documentation of the Jury proceedings and his professional counsel on the development of this publication.

In addition to those who worked on this publication, there were many individuals involved with other aspects of the competition, from the development of the program to the planning of the exhibition this publication accompanies. My thanks to the members of the Technical Review Panel— Tom Mangan, Kongal Guellec, Frank Sanchis, Marty Goldman, Bruce McDonell, Peter Casler, Linda S. Ferber, and Dan Weidmann—who contributed many hours of hard work before the Jury convened.

Historical building plans pertaining to The Brooklyn Museum are located in several repositories throughout New York City. I am most grateful to the staffs at the New-York Historical Society and the Art Commission of the City of New York for their generous cooperation in providing the competitors access to these documents.

Individuals at many institutions assisted us in our research, including Nanette Smith, Art Commission of the City of New York; Terry Ariano, Museum of the City of

New York; Nina Rutenberg, New-York Historical Society; Evan Kingsley, Olmsted Historic Site; Cheryl Leibold, The Pennsylvania Academy of the Fine Arts; and Richard Moylan, Greenwood Cemetery. For sharing their insights on William Lescaze, we would like to thank Carolyn Davis, Lescaze Archives, Syracuse University, and Lindsay Shapiro, Lorraine Lanmon, and Lee Lescaze. Helene Fried, San Francisco Museum of Modern Art, and Jonathan Green, Ohio State University, freely shared their experience in producing competition publications. Michael Crosby, American Institute of Architects, and Daralice Boles, *Progressive Architecture,* were helpful in locating photographs.

I particularly appreciate the professionalism of Nathaniel Lieberman and Cervin Robinson, who photographed respectively the architectural models and boards. Rosanna Liebman's organizational abilities were invaluable during the photography. Tim Druckrey did a superb job of printing the historical photographs.

I extend my thanks to the team at Rizzoli who worked with us on this publication—Solveig Williams, Managing Editor, Charles Davey, Production Manager, Alessandro Franchini, Designer, and Jane Fluegel, Senior Editor.

Each member of The Brooklyn Museum staff is in some way responsible for the successful completion of any project, but I would especially like to thank Roy R. Eddey, Deputy Director, Linda S. Ferber, Chief Curator, and members of the curatorial staff for their effort in developing the competition building program; Gwen Glass, Capital Construction Manager, for recording and translating the Jury proceedings with professional precision; Dan Weidmann, Vice Director for Operations, and Sylvester Yavana, Assistant Capital Construction Manager, for the design and installation of the Jury room; Bob Hajek, Assistant, Design Department, for patiently processing our many demands for photographic services; William Lyall, Chief Photographer, and Howard Ferrara, Senior Lab Technician, for expediting those orders; Deborah Wythe, Archivist, for suggesting avenues for research; Richard Waller, Chief Designer, for solving many arcane problems; Jeffrey Strean, Exhibition Designer, for his thoughtful and sensitive design of the exhibition; Elaine Koss, Managing Editor, and John Antonides, Editor, for their patience and adeptness in editing the text; and Rena Zurofsky, Vice Director for Marketing Services, for serving as our liaison with Rizzoli. I am also grateful to the carpenters, painters, electricians, and art handlers for their skillful installation of the exhibition. I want to give a special thanks to Deirdre Lawrence, Principal Librarian, for her invaluable assistance. We were able to benefit from her extensive study of the Museum's history for the development of both the competition program and the publication.

The dedication, patience, and energy of the Planning Office staff pulled this project together. From the project's beginning, my assistant, Wanda Sweat, bravely took on the challenge of the computer to process all the manuscripts in addition to her many other duties; Emma Lewis, volunteer, dedicated her summer to the reproduction and coordination of the Museum's historical photographs; and Mary Beth Betts, Special Projects Coordinator, turned chaos into order: to all a special thanks.

To Bailey Van Hook, Research Associate and my right hand, who took on the responsibility of coordinating the many details that a publication and exhibition entail, from gathering photographs to expediting manuscripts with fastidiousness, care, and initiative, I am indeed indebted.

Lastly, I am most appreciative for the experience of working on a project of such significance, and I want to thank Robert T. Buck, Director, for giving me this extraordinary opportunity.

Joan Darragh
Vice Director for Planning
The Brooklyn Museum

Introduction
Reyner Banham

The competition for the design of a program of extensions and completions at The Brooklyn Museum has come at a significant juncture in the history of architecture. The past quarter century has seen an accelerating rise in the level of both expectation and accomplishment in the design of art galleries and museums. Indeed, the last decade, since the opening of the Centre National d'Art et de Culture Georges Pompidou in Paris in 1977 (fig. 1), has been one of quite unprecedented activity that has left the traditional concept of an art museum both radically questioned and triumphantly reaffirmed—sometimes in one and the same building, as in the case of James Stirling's remarkable extensions to the old Staatsgalerie in Stuttgart.

In these processes of challenge and affirmation, the physical body of The Brooklyn Museum stood, at the time of the decision to hold the competition, in a proud position in the history of both developments (fig. 2). The original 1893 design by McKim, Mead & White was one of the last and most accomplished examples of the established Neoclassical tradition that sprang from Karl-Friedrich Schinkel's Altes Museum of 1823 in Berlin and Charles Smirke's slightly later British Museum in London. It was a tradition that had done noble service in establishing not only standards of gallery accommodation within but also an acceptably gracious stylistic representation without: it had made the art museum a respectable member of the family of architectural types.

Precisely because it was so acceptable, established, and a classic of its kind, an example like The Brooklyn Museum could not help appearing elitist and undemocratic to the reforming zealots of the 1930s. A more "user-friendly" approach was deemed proper to the times, and in 1934 the grand flight of ceremonial steps leading up to the portico on the main front facing Eastern Parkway was demolished, and the present entrances were created at grade level, heading straight into the vast William Lescaze–inspired ground-floor lobby. While it is currently fashionable to denounce this alteration as insensitive vandalism, it was a gesture of

1

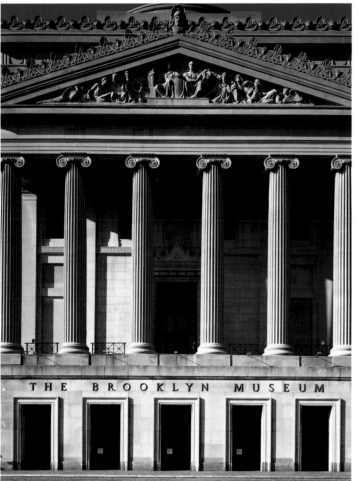

2

historic importance, heralding new concepts of museum operation and public address. Indeed, the reforms begun in the thirties give the Museum a better claim to the title "the first modern museum" than even Edward Durell Stone and Philip Goodwin's central block of The Museum of Modern Art complex on 53rd Street in New York. These reforms were a radical critique of all the assumptions underlying the Neoclassical typologies of the accepted treasure-house style of museum design. The challenge was clear: from that time on, the traditional museum was under notice, and the recent rediscovery and reaffirmation of the tradition's forgotten virtues cannot reverse the process then set in motion, but only modify it.

Nevertheless, in more recent years there have been some unexpected diversions and changes of direction. The seemingly unhaltable trend toward more flexible and highly serviced display spaces, promised by Louis Kahn's Yale University Art Gallery of 1953 and finally delivered by the Centre Pompidou some twenty years later, came to a notable halt just as the Centre opened; the long-sought ideal of total flexibility, of wide-open spaces unencumbered with architecture, had proved too relentlessly demanding for both curators and display designers. However, the expected replacement of this trend with a return to stylistic classicism (or even some Post-Modernist version of it) and to traditional gallery types has failed to materialize.

The designs that were selected for Helen Searing's exhibition *New American Art Museums* at the Whitney Museum of American Art, New York, in 1982, proved to be an extraordinarily mixed bag; although stylistically diverse in the faces they offered to the public street and notably uncertain about the proper forms of gallery spaces, they were in general agreement in calling for vastly more curatorial and laboratory space than their sponsors could believe possible. Those that have actually been built range from Henry Cobb's urbane, but contrived, Portland (Maine) Museum of Art, with its basically traditional top-lit galleries, to Richard

19

Meier's High Museum of Art in Atlanta (fig. 3), a grand and distinguished exercise in Modernist-revival styling, but with gallery spaces little different from the types long since established by The Museum of Modern Art in New York (and as disappointing as Cesar Pelli's recent alterations there).

Of all the projects exhibited at the Whitney, the most successful as built is probably the Dallas Museum of Art, by Edward Larrabee Barnes, though it suffers from a certain blandness caused by an extreme reticence in the detailing. Not even the Dallas Museum, however, has proven to be the "art gallery for the eighties" promised in Searing's subtitle, for the eighties have turned out to be even more surprising than the best-informed trend-spotters and museum-watchers could have anticipated.

Two events, more than any others, have changed the nature and direction of museum design. The first was the entry (or reentry) of the J. Paul Getty Trust into the museum-building business in 1982. Its search for an architect to build a new center to house its rapidly growing collections differs from the program of other American museums in the sheer extravagance of the money involved, inviting higher-flying design concepts than had been entertained since the confident late nineteenth century. Moreover, the mode of search by an elaborate system of consultancy and visitation of completed buildings, rather than by a competition, encouraged a more deliberate yet flexible selection process than before, apparently leaving its mark, for instance, on the early stages of the search for The Brooklyn Museum's new architects. And finally, the willingness of the Getty to cast the nets of choice worldwide, so that its short list contained an American, a Japanese, and a Briton, opened up the American argument to far-flung influences that had had no part in Searing's conspectus of 1982.

If the Getty's final choice, Richard Meier, seemed a shade too predictable, the sense of anticlimax was largely caused by a closely related but originally unconnected event that

occurred just as the selection process was nearing its end: the opening of James Stirling's Neue Staatsgalerie in Stuttgart (fig. 4). Given his international eminence, Stirling would probably have made the Getty short list in any event, but Stuttgart made him a very hot contender (and the preferred candidate among most of the museum professionals involved in the search). In retrospect, the Stuttgart design seems to have altered the museum-architecture rule book almost as much as the Getty Trust itself had done.

The previous modern paradigm for such extensions to Neoclassical museums had been established in 1962, when Gordon Bunshaft's extremely intelligent "Knox" wing was added to E. B. Green and William Wicks's then sixty-year-old "Albright" building in Buffalo, forming the celebrated Albright-Knox Art Gallery. Although Bunshaft's black-glass pavilion is unapologetically defiant of the earlier building's crisp Neoclassicism, the two are craftily united by a marble base that continues the line of the basement story of the original structure. Such a contrast was as proper to the spirit of the times as was the removal of the steps from the portico of The Brooklyn Museum thirty years earlier, and it was also as appropriate to the site and to the nature and needs of the institution.

Stirling showed at Stuttgart that such neat dichotomies were no longer necessary, that in the architecturally so-

3

4

phisticated eighties one could be modern and traditional at the same time without sacrificing the virtues of either and still deliver the large volumes of auxiliary public spaces that a major museum now needs to support its galleries. But where Stuttgart really "raised the ante" was in giving museum building committees the idea that they could expect a work of genius from their chosen architects!

Not all Stirling's museum work is of such quality, but the general judgment on Stuttgart is that he achieved at the very least a level of brilliance not seen anywhere else in the present decade. Such quality may not be within the compass of all architects; nor is it deserved by all building committees nor possible on all sites. But the Neue Staatsgalerie offered an example, set a standard, suggested a vocabulary even, for resolving almost exactly the kinds of problems posed by the extension of The Brooklyn Museum. These circumstances made Stirling an appropriate, indeed a necessary, choice for a juror, even if he was not available as a competitor, in the final selection for the Museum.

In his design of galleries at Stuttgart, Stirling had shown a mixture of adaptability, sensitivity, and boldness that is peculiarly appropriate to the tasks at both Stuttgart and Brooklyn. Although the galleries in Stuttgart have an apparently traditional top-lit section and are arranged in a seemingly conventional manner around a rectangular courtyard, they are proportionately wider and lower than the Neoclassical norm, making them better adapted to the display of modern art, or to the modern display of older art.

The relation of the galleries to the courtyard departs from the older convention as well, since the court is not a significant means of entry to the galleries. Instead, the visitor enters the sequence of display spaces from either end and by spectacular ascents from below, an entirely Modernist concept, as is Stirling's whole procedure of stacking the rest of the accommodations on the site, with the galleries as the crown of a set of terraces containing all the auxiliary accommodations.

3. Richard Meier & Partners, High Museum of Art, Atlanta, 1983 (Courtesy of Richard Meier & Partners).
4. James Stirling Michael Wilford and Associates, Neue Staatsgalerie, Stuttgart, 1985 (Courtesy of Arcaid).

Clearly, Stirling received great advantages, as well as severe challenges, from the steep but ample site alongside the original Staatsgalerie, which enabled him to build as it were a "Musée Parallele." Thomas Beeby, to make an obvious comparison to both Stuttgart and Brooklyn, has had equal challenges, but fewer advantages, in the task of completing the seemingly endless extension of Shepley, Rutan & Coolidge's serenely Classical Art Institute of Chicago back over the Illinois Central tracks to Lake Shore Drive. Although the result may be everything that Post-Modernist sensitivity to high Beaux-Arts Classicism can make it, the difficult and constricted site does not afford Beeby the chance to deliver large historical gestures on a fundamentally Modernist plan, as Stirling has done. Successful or not, these ingenious exercises in extension behind powerful facades have left interesting and obvious challenges on the drafting tables of the architects involved in the Brooklyn competition—as well as some valuable hints on how to tackle them.

Another factor in any consideration of museum design in the middle eighties—a matter that has also changed the rules of the game—is the sharply increasing professionalism of museum staffs and their own enhanced awareness of it. Though the massive organizational self-examination undertaken by The Brooklyn Museum staff as part of the preparation for the Museum's architectural competition is of itself a landmark in the process of professionalization, parallel if dissimilar developments can be seen elsewhere in the eighties. For instance, the new galleries for the Menil Collection in Houston required that Renzo Piano (co-architect with Richard Rogers of the Centre Pompidou) design a facility in which the square footage of curatorial, administrative, studio, and technical spaces (not to mention the lecture hall) would outnumber that of the gallery space by a factor of perhaps three to one, without distracting from what must always be the main and essential function of an art museum: to bring artworks and the public together to their mutual advantage. If the schedule of accommodations specified for 21 the Menil represents "the revenge of the professionals," Piano's subtly understated design has answered the challenge with equal professionalism. Though constrained by the special considerations of the unique suburban cityscape in which the Menil is located, Piano still had the obvious advantage of a flat, clear, and unencumbered site on which to dispose the elements of his design as expansively as seemed fit.

No such advantage attends the task of designing extensions to The Brooklyn Museum, and even the often-assumed benefit of the new work all being at the back of the main structure, away from the public gaze, may be only an illusory advantage. Quite apart from the encumbrance of the site by extensions, additions, subsidiary structures, and parking lot, as well as the remains of a grand axial layout of the Botanic Garden beyond, the ground is haunted by the unrequited intentions of the original McKim, Mead & White project, the whole range of unbuilt galleries and their facades that would have completed, balanced, and complemented the rhetoric of the Museum's front. Architects may choose to defy those articulate ghosts, but none can ignore them.

These "encumbrances," more than those of any other site, are reasons why the whole extraordinary recent history of museum design works to the advantage of the Brooklyn project. The most considerable talents to have worked on museum design of late—not only Stirling at Stuttgart but also Charles Moore at the Dartmouth College Hood Museum of Art, I. M. Pei at the Museum of Fine Arts, Boston, and Cobb at the Portland Museum—have worked precisely on the extension or completion of existing structures of distinct and demanding character; indeed, one could almost propose a sustained tradition of such work that extends back at least to Venturi, Rauch and Scott Brown's addition to the Allen Memorial Art Museum at Oberlin College in 1973 (fig. 5). In the process, the profession has accumulated a body of skills and a wealth of experience that ultimately count for more than mere changes of fashion or Post-Modernist fancies about Neoclassicism. One can only be struck by the fact

that the winning proposal by Arata Isozaki and James Stewart Polshek for The Brooklyn Museum is not one of those entries that attempted in one way or another to be "in keeping" with the stylistic aspects of the McKim, Mead & White design or to produce a neo-Neoclassicism out of a supposed deference to the original.

Rather, Isozaki and Polshek have executed some very bold moves that demonstrate how the legacy of Modernism makes possible a sympathetic critique of the rigidities of Neoclassicism without anywhere failing to respect that honorable and serviceable tradition (fig. 6). The grand galleries of the original design, vast as Roman baths, and the functionalist spaces of later additions will be supplemented, not replaced. A subtly varied set of new galleries, somewhat traditional in their sections and lighting, but of more compact and manageable dimensions, will pack a lot of desperately needed wall space for artworks into a fairly modest total envelope.

The line of Washington Avenue, The Brooklyn Museum's crucial secondary means of entrance, will now be honored; the fan shape of the new auditorium will allow for the alignment of the proposed sculpture garden parallel with the street. The relentless rectangularity of the original design could not have accommodated this alignment, yet the pretext, the "hinge," for doing so is provided by the circular portico originally proposed for that site. Similarly, the long and closely packed box of galleries to the west will respect the line of the McKim, Mead & White design and, while making no attempt to reproduce the Classical orders of the original over the whole facade, will still match the existing corner pavilion of the Parkway elevation and bring the new facade to a fitting rearward conclusion.

Finally, it is possible that the unavoidably controversial giant obelisk proposed for the center of the new rear elevation will look even better than the gigantic dome that had originally been proposed for that location, while the space underneath it will echo the columnar Classicism of the other

22

5. Venturi, Rauch and Scott Brown, Allen Memorial Art Museum, Oberlin College, Oberlin, Ohio, 1973 (Courtesy of Venturi, Rauch and Scott Brown).
6. Arata Isozaki & Associates and James Stewart Polshek and Partners, The Brooklyn Museum Master Plan, perspective view looking up into obelisk, 1986.

ceremonial spaces within the existing structure. And, yes, the steps to the portico will indeed be replaced. The lesson of these last twenty years of experience that the winning design seems to have learned is that powerful designs require, and deserve, powerful responses, and that the most necessary and valuable of the museum-design skills accumulated by the architectural profession are concerned with the points where powerful old work and the powerful new join or confront one another.

But let it not be forgotten that the new work involved is not—nor has it been in any of the examples cited above— a purely, or even predominantly, aesthetic exercise. Modern museum budgets and current operating procedures, even more than those of the past, demand that every square foot of new floor space be *usable* and that every undercroft and attic be capable of working for its living.

The level of performance expected of modern museum buildings, and especially the level of performance *per dollar*, begins to challenge the standards traditionally set by industrial construction and must appear quite modest beside the expenditure accepted in some recent office structures such as Richard Rogers's Lloyds of London. The idea that monuments of culture are somehow excused the kind of economic discipline that governs the rest of modern life is one of the reasons that "Culture" is so often felt to be divorced from "Real Life"; yet a close reading of the quarter century of new museums and museum extensions that leads up to the Brooklyn competition reveals few examples of waste or excess. Rather, we have seen some extraordinary achievements in creating works of dignity and enlightenment out of resources that would have caused most architects of the past to resign the commission. The best museum architects of today are made of sterner stuff, and The Brooklyn Museum may therefore count itself fortunate.

23

Part I. History

1. McKim, Mead & White and The Brooklyn Museum, 1893–1934
Leland M. Roth

The imposing Museum designed by McKim, Mead & White for The Brooklyn Institute of Arts and Sciences in the 1890s was conceived as the crowning cultural achievement of the sister city to New York. Yet even as the Museum was designed, the status of Brooklyn as an independent city was nearing an end. The first section of the Museum was hardly built and opened to the public when Brooklyn as a sovereign municipal entity ceased to exist and became part of New York City. Thus, the symbolism of The Brooklyn Museum as the embodiment of Brooklyn was undercut almost from the beginning. Nonetheless, in the last few years that heroic beginning has taken on new meaning. The story of the creation of The Brooklyn Museum, like the story of its current revitalization, is one of high social and educational purpose.

Brooklyn Arises

After purchasing Manhattan Island from the Indians in 1626, the Dutch began to establish settlements on what they called Lange Eylandt (Long Island). The first of these was Nieuw Amersfoort, begun in 1636 at the west end of Jamaica Bay. Later called Flatlands, this community lay on the east side of the long glacial moraine that runs like a spine through the center of western Long Island. Ten years later Breuckelen (Brooklyn) was established on the west side of that glacial moraine, on a rise that overlooked the East River and New Amsterdam. In the next few years Brooklyn in turn was surrounded by four additional villages in what is now Kings County—Bushwick, Flatbush, New Utrecht, and Gravesend. During the eighteenth century, while New York took on the character of a busy trading and administrative center, Brooklyn and the other scattered settlements on western Long Island retained a far more rural aspect; except for their village centers, these were farm communities. As these nodes of agricultural settlement grew, the village boundaries neared each other. In 1816 Brooklyn was incorporated by the state as a village, and in 1834 it became a city.

Brooklynites were proud of their separate status and were

1.1. Plan of Prospect Park, Brooklyn, New York, 1871, Olmsted Vaux & Co., Landscape Architects. This version of the park plan, originally laid out by Calvert Vaux in 1865, shows the triangle for museums labeled "ground reserved for public buildings," the Mount Prospect Reservoir, and several proposed landscaped parkways extending out from the park. The curved roadway reaching eastward from Grand Army Plaza, here labeled "Jamaica Park Way," was later renamed Eastern Parkway. This drawing also contains proposals for extension of the reservoir and landscaping in the area where The Brooklyn Museum was started in 1895 (Courtesy of the Brooklyn Historical Society).

careful to preserve their rural identity. In 1833 General Jeremiah Johnson of Brooklyn claimed that the East River would always separate New York and Brooklyn and "must forever continue to form an unsurmountable obstacle to their union."[1] Of course, even before Johnson wrote this, the two cities had long been linked economically: as early as 1642, more than two centuries before John A. Roebling's bridge spanned the supposed "unsurmountable obstacle," ferries had begun carrying commuters back and forth to Manhattan. Roebling's famous bridge simply provided a more dependable all-weather link between the two cities, making their interdependence more visible and their mutually distinctive qualities more pronounced. Brooklyn was "New York's bedroom," a city of homes and churches.[2]

Creating the Site

Although numerically the population of Brooklyn was less than New York's, the rate of population increase was far greater in Brooklyn—between 1830 and 1860 the number of Manhattan residents grew from 202,589 to 813,660, whereas the population of Brooklyn jumped from 15,394 to 266,661.[3] In 1850 Brooklyn was the third largest American city, and by 1890, although surpassed by the exploding Chicago, it would still be the fourth largest.

The need for setting aside public lands in Manhattan led to the creation of Central Park and brought its designers, Frederick Law Olmsted and Calvert Vaux, to the forefront of the new profession of landscape architecture. As early as the 1850s Brooklyn civic leaders such as James S.T. Stranahan urged that a similar park be set aside in Brooklyn. In 1860 the city purchased a parcel of 320 acres at a site then at the far southern edge of built-up Brooklyn, where the streets ran up against the glacial moraine and Mount Prospect.

Calvert Vaux devised the first preliminary plan for Prospect Park in 1865 while Olmsted was in California.[4] Although the broad, irregular site for Brooklyn's new park was more promising as a picturesque landscape than the long narrow rectangle of Central Park had been, it was cut through by Flatbush Avenue, a major thoroughfare (fig. 1.1). Since Vaux anticipated that the principal entrance to the new park would be at the sharp corner of Flatbush Avenue and what became Prospect Park West, he and Olmsted proposed that the triangle of park property between Flatbush and Washington avenues be set aside for "Museums and Other Educational Edifices."[5] The larger remaining parcel on the west side of Flatbush Avenue could then be developed solely as a park preserve, obviating any demands for building sites within Prospect Park as had already become a vexing problem in Central Park. Vaux also successfully persuaded the city fathers to purchase additional lots to create the oval Grand Army Plaza, forming the principal northern entrance to the new park.

To Olmsted and Vaux, urban parks were not merely isolated oases of green but rather larger elements in integrated networks of public landscaped spaces. The parks themselves were to be connected by linear, parklike roads that would provide gracious and restorative means of movement through the city. If Olmsted and Vaux experienced difficulties in getting their parks built according to plan, they had even less success in persuading governing bodies to create these landscaped boulevards connecting public recreational lands. But they succeeded first in Brooklyn.

In their report on Prospect Park of 1866, Olmsted and Vaux discussed the idea of landscaped boulevards leading out from the park, although they did not include such a boulevard in the published plan of the park dated 1866–67.[6] This concept was more fully developed in their subsequent report of 1868, as well as in a separate publication, "Observations on the Progress of Improvements in Street Plans, with Special Reference to The Parkway Proposed to Be Laid out in Brooklyn," of the same year.[7] In this report they described in detail the design of a "parkway"—a word they invented—consisting of a broad thoroughfare combining a

28

wide central carriageway, flanking walks, and side roads for local traffic, all separated by six wide bands of shrubs and trees; altogether, from the fronts of the house lots on one side to those on the other, the parkway was to be 260 feet wide. In 1870–74 Brooklyn's Eastern Parkway was laid out following this design, running from the east side of the oval plaza at the entrance to Prospect Park (passing north of Mount Prospect and the city reservoir), and extending to Ralph Avenue, then the city limit.

Meanwhile the entrances to Prospect Park were sharply defined by the Classical architectural pavilions and stanchions designed by McKim, Mead & White, so that the environment around Prospect Park demonstrated something of the character celebrated in the Court of Honor at the World's Columbian Exposition in Chicago in 1893 (figs. 1.2, 1.4). Particularly imposing was the massive memorial arch by John H. Duncan built in the middle of the Grand Army Plaza oval in 1889–92.

Although Brooklyn was beginning to achieve the urban grandeur being created in New York by McKim, Mead & White, there were those who were convinced that its full economic potential could be achieved only through union with New York. Early proposals for amalgamation had been voiced by Brooklynites in 1827 and again in 1868, but in 1887 Andrew H. Green undertook a serious effort to effect this merger. So successful were his efforts that by 1892 a group of prominent and vociferous Brooklyn residents joined to oppose his plan. Even the Brooklyn *Eagle*, the prominent newspaper that had extolled construction of Roebling's East River bridge, now vigorously argued against the annexation of Brooklyn by New York, for its editors "dreaded the end of an independent existence for Brooklyn."[8] But the movement for consolidation advanced nonetheless, and final unification of the five boroughs to form Greater New York took place in January 1898.

Creation of The Brooklyn Institute

One of the visible symbols of Brooklyn's rapidly disappearing independent existence was The Brooklyn Institute of Arts and Sciences (fig. 1.3). The Institute had its origin in the Apprentices' Library, organized in 1823 to bring "the benefits of knowledge to that portion of our youth who are engaged in learning the mechanical arts" with the aim of making them "useful and respectable members of society."[9] Like Benjamin Franklin's Apprentices' Library in Philadelphia, after which it was modeled, the Brooklyn Library was intended to improve the moral character of the working classes. But it was more than a place for reading, for the original charter also called for collecting "books, maps, drawing apparatus, models of machinery, tools and implements generally."[10] Thus the Library was meant from the start to be a general educational institution, serving the broadest public by gathering a wide range of objects as aids to education and the improvement of life.

Initially the Library was housed in a small, rented frame house at 143 Fulton Street, but by 1825 growth necessitated construction of a special building at Henry and Cranberry streets (fig. 1.5). This was a vernacular building, not so different in size or character from contemporaneous local residences in what is now called the Federal style of architecture.[11]

Throughout its life, the institution flourished under the care and direction of individuals committed to its educational purpose. One of its early champions was Augustus Graham, who was instrumental in enlisting public support in the mid-1830s. With use increasing and the collections growing, expanded quarters again had to be found, and in 1841 the Library was offered space in the imposing Neoclassical building erected by the Brooklyn Lyceum at Washington and Concord streets (fig. 1.6). The educational activities, public lectures, and collections continued to increase and broaden in scope, as indicated by its change of name to The Brooklyn Institute in 1843.[12]

1.2

1.3

1.4

1.2. Soldiers' and Sailors' Memorial Arch and entrance to Prospect Park, looking over reservoir toward completed Brooklyn Institute, circa 1915 (Courtesy of The Library of Congress).

1.3. The Brooklyn Institute of Arts and Sciences, view from southeast, circa 1910 (Courtesy of the Museum of the City of New York).

1.4. View of Court of Honor, World's Columbian Exposition, Chicago, with Agriculture Building by McKim, Mead & White (Courtesy of Chicago Historical Society).

In 1881 a fire destroyed part of the Washington Street building. Although repairs were made, interest in the institution was again slipping, until General John B. Woodward made its development his personal concern. It was Woodward who selected Franklin W. Hooper to become the new Director of The Brooklyn Institute in 1889.[13] As the Rev. John W. Chadwick put it, Woodward and Hooper effectively raised The Brooklyn Institute from the dead.[14] In the next several years the Institute was reorganized into a number of individual departments, many of them formed as various Brooklyn scientific and educational societies were absorbed into the Institute. Hooper's vision of the mission of the expanded Institute appeared in *The First Year Book*:

The nucleus of a broad and comprehensive institution for the advancement of science and art, . . . laboring not only for the advancement of knowledge, but also for the education of the people through lectures and collections in art and science. . . . It was felt that Brooklyn should have an Institute of Arts and Sciences worthy of her wealth, her position, her culture, and her people.[15]

Within a year the Institute had been completely restructured, and in April 1890 it was reincorporated by the State of New York as The Brooklyn Institute of Arts and Sciences, with sixteen separate departments that eventually grew to twenty-seven.[16] The organizational basis of a great and multifaceted educational institution had been created.

Woodward and Hooper's ambitious plans clearly exceeded the capacity of the old Neoclassical building on Washington Street. A new building would be required, and in June 1889 the city of Brooklyn took the first official steps to set aside the land on either side of the Mount Prospect reservoir as a reserve for "art and science museums and libraries."[17] A Citizens' Committee had already been formulating the objectives of the proposed expanded Institute of Arts and Sciences. In their report, published in February 1890, the committee acknowledged that the scope of the proposed institution surpassed anything yet attempted in the United States. They had studied the Museum of Comparative Zoology at Harvard University organized by Louis Agassiz as well as the National Museum in Washington, the National Gallery in London, the Louvre in Paris, the Museum of Natural History at South Kensington, London, and the Museums of Practical Arts in Berlin and Paris. In contrast to all these, they concluded, the new structure required for The Brooklyn Institute of Arts and Sciences had to be built

upon a plan far different from that which now prevails in the great majority of such buildings. While the buildings should be of indestructible material and of commanding proportions, they should be so constructed in their interior arrangements, as to be easily capable of allowing the classification and reclassification of materials, as the collections grow.[18]

The problem that Woodward, the Institute Trustees, and the Citizens' Committee faced was that there were no other museums anywhere that combined, in such a systematic and educational way, the whole spectrum of human achievement as was being proposed for Brooklyn. The expanded Institute was to advance human knowledge "in all departments of art and science" and to provide in one facility what the Lowell Institute, the Society of Natural History, and the art museum provided for Boston, what the Franklin Institute, the Academy of Science, and the Gallery of Fine Arts provided for Philadelphia, and what The Metropolitan Museum of Art and the American Museum of Natural History provided for New York.[19]

The large public museum was essentially an invention of the nineteenth century, the preeminent period of collecting, cataloguing, and presenting all manner of objects—animal,

1.5

vegetable, and mineral.[20] Important museums presenting specialized collections included the South Kensington decorative arts museum in London (now the Victoria and Albert Museum), begun in 1856; the American Museum of Natural History, created in New York in 1869 and housed in the first section of a large Romanesque building by J. Cleveland Cady; and, for the display of machines and scientific apparatus, the Smithsonian Institution in Washington, D.C., housed in the famous red Romanesque building on the Mall built in 1846–55 by James Renwick. Museums of painting and sculpture were even more in evidence. Between 1840 and 1890 in the United States, major public art museums were built in Hartford, Philadelphia, Boston, and New York, all of them housed in Gothic-inspired buildings.[21]

As the new building for The Brooklyn Institute of Arts and Sciences was being planned, projects were also underway for large Classical museums of the fine arts in Chicago, Washington, D.C., and Pittsburgh.[22] But of them all, American and European, The Brooklyn Museum was to be unique, for in its halls were to be displayed, in scientifically ordered ranges, every kind of artifact of human creativity and invention, the full record of the rise of the human species, presented to promote public education and visual delight—nothing less than the whole of human experience. As Franklin Hooper said when the cornerstone was laid in December 1895, the Museum was to embrace "all known human history, the infinite capacity of man to act, to think, and to love, and the many departments of science and of art which he has developed. Through its collections in the arts and sciences, and through its libraries it should be possible to read the history of the world."[23]

Building The Brooklyn Institute

As it happened, the concept of the expansive Brooklyn Institute of Arts and Sciences was developed at a moment in American history when city officials had begun to think of urban rebuilding on a grand and coherent scale. In 1892–93, as the Institute Trustees developed a scheme for conducting a tiered competition to obtain the design for the new building, the most accomplished American architects (including New York's McKim, Mead & White) were gathered in Chicago to design the largest international exposition the United States had ever mounted. What they wanted to present to the world was an image of refined architectural order and urban coherence. The result was the carefully proportioned spatial and architectural environment of the 1893 World's Columbian Exposition (fig. 1.4). The Exposition inspired scores of cities across the country to create ordered civic centers, giving rise to the City Beautiful movement; it implanted the idea that architecture, richly embellished with painting and sculpture, served the public good in the most direct and visible way. Solidly built and judiciously ornamented Classicism would be good public policy. In Brooklyn, McKim, Mead & White had already begun to advance that view in their entrances to Prospect Park; very shortly they were to be given a far grander opportunity in their design for the new Brooklyn Institute.

The movement to build a new museum for the Institute began in December 1888, when a public meeting was announced in 1,500 letters sent out to Brooklyn citizens. At the meeting in February 1889, community leaders spoke of the need for an imposing building befitting the growing importance of the Institute and Brooklyn and of the "educating and uplifting influence" that art exerts on rich and poor alike.[24] They also observed that a splendid building would benefit the schools and make Brooklyn an even more attractive city in which to live, thereby increasing real estate values. A committee of twenty-five was appointed to work with Institute Trustees and the Director in the design of the new museum.

The committee's first action was to promote passage of state legislation in 1889 enabling the city of Brooklyn to set aside the triangle around the Mount Prospect reservoir for construction of "museums of art and science and li-

33

1.5. Brooklyn Apprentices' Library at Henry and Cranberry streets, Brooklyn, 1825–26.
1.6. The Brooklyn Lyceum, Washington Street.

1.6

braries.'' The next step, in 1890, was legal reorganization of the old Institute as the new and more encompassing Brooklyn Institute of Arts and Sciences.[25] The governing board of the reorganized Institute then secured passage of state legislation providing for construction by the city of Brooklyn at a cost of $300,000 of a museum building to be leased to the Institute for 100 years for a nominal annual fee.[26] There was a condition, however, that the $300,000 (to be raised by the sale of city bonds) was to be matched by $200,000 raised by the Institute. Meanwhile, the old building on Washington Street was sold to the city (it was later demolished to make way for enlarged approaches to the Brooklyn Bridge), and the collections moved to temporary quarters. With the proceeds of that sale, plus subscriptions for the new building, reserves by the end of 1890 reached $190,906, only $9,094 short of the required sum; early in 1891 the funds gathered by the Institute surpassed the required minimum. During 1891 the Mayor and Brooklyn Park Commissioners set aside the actual site for the Museum—a parcel of 11.9 acres southeast of the Mount Prospect reservoir fronting on Eastern Parkway and extending to Washington Avenue (fig. 1.7).

The remaining step was to obtain a suitable design for the new building. In keeping with the democratic character of the institution, the Advisory Board to the Institute's Department of Architecture decided in December 1892 to sponsor a two-tier competition. The first stage would be open to the members of the Institute's Department of Architecture, many of them young men beginning their careers; the second stage would be limited to seven contestants— four architects invited by the Mayor and Park Commissioners at the recommendation of Trustees of the Institute, together with the three winners from the first stage of the competition. The seven participants in this second stage were to be paid $500 to cover the expenses of developing their designs. This somewhat complex arrangement was created to mollify the objections of many prominent architects who refused to participate in competitions because results were often rigged in favor of political favorites and the resulting buildings constructed with little regard to the plans awarded the prize.[27] During the final judging, the names of the architects were to be covered over, so that individual personalities would not come into play in awarding the commission. The jury appointed to make the award consisted of Professor A. D. F. Hamlin of the School of Architecture at Columbia University, the prominent architect Robert S. Peabody of Boston, and architect George L. Morse of Brooklyn; it was this trio, together with Director Hooper, William B. Tubby, head of the Institute's Department of Architecture, and Charles T. Mott, who had drawn up the program requirements for the new Museum during 1892, including the judgment of the Trustees that the style of the Museum be Classic.[28]

Letters of invitation to architects were sent out during October 1892, and copies of the first stage of the competition program were circulated early in January 1893. Twenty members of the Institute's Department of Architecture participated in the first stage, including William B. Bigelow and James L. Cromwell, Jr. (fig. 1.8).[29] Of these, the three selected to continue to the second stage were the young Brooklyn architects Cromwell, Albert L. Brockway, and William A. Boring, who had recently been an assistant in the office of McKim, Mead & White.[30] The participating professionals in the second stage of the competition included J. Cleveland Cady (architect of the Brooklyn Academy of Design and the American Museum of Natural History), Carrère & Hastings (who in a few years would win the competition for the New York Public Library), the Parfitt Brothers (prominent Brooklyn architects), and McKim, Mead & White. Each was to submit seven mounted ink drawings on boards measuring 36 by 44 inches.

On May 19, 1893, the Trustees heard the jury's report favoring design number six; when its identification block was revealed, it was discovered to be the work of McKim, Mead & White (fig. 1.9). In view of the scale and unprec-

1.7. Site map of area surrounding The Brooklyn Institute, circa 1898, showing proposed museum building and portion completed by 1927 (L.M. Roth, adapted from Hyde atlas of Brooklyn, 1898).

1.8. James L. Cromwell, Jr., perspective (top), and William B. Bigelow, plan, competition entries for The Brooklyn Institute of Arts and Sciences (Courtesy of the Museum of the City of New York).

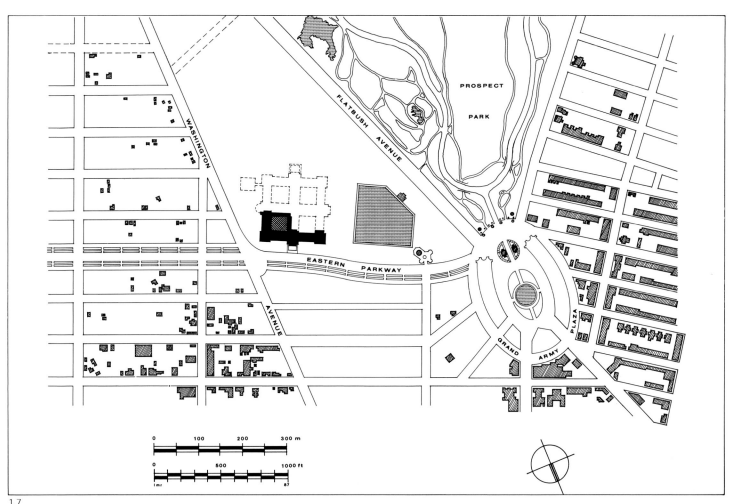

1.7

1.8

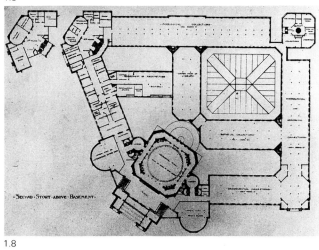

1.8

1.9

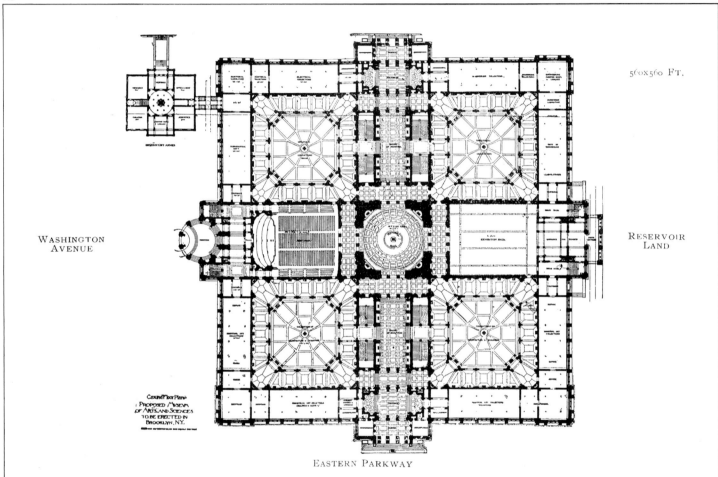

WASHINGTON
AVENUE

560X560 FT.

RESERVOIR
LAND

EASTERN PARKWAY

1.10

1.11

edented complexity of the problem, it is not surprising that there remained deficiencies in McKim, Mead & White's solution. The jury recommended that the firm confer with the Trustees to work out the remaining problems.[31] Several days later all the submitted drawings were on public display at the temporary headquarters of the Institute on Montague Street and were described at length in the Brooklyn *Eagle*.[32]

The winners of the competition were at the forefront of their profession. Having begun their practice in 1879, McKim, Mead & White had won acclaim for the remarkably elegant yet restrained housing group they built on Madison Avenue in New York for the railroad developer Henry Villard (1882–85). This achievement in turn helped win for them the commission for the building of the Boston Public Library (1887–95), a structure that established a new character for urban public buildings in the United States for the next half century.[33] By 1892 they operated the largest private architectural office in the world, training scores of young men who went on to distinguished careers. One of these young assistants, Egerton Swartwout, in writing of those days, revealed how the firm handled competition projects. The Brooklyn Institute, he recalled, was a project handled by partner Charles Follen McKim, although Garry Hewlett and Austin Lord worked up McKim's preliminary sketches.

The plan made more of an impression on me than the elevations [Swartwout recalled]. *At first they built only one wing of it and that was worked up by Phil Sawyer, good and simple but too large in scale for the location; the building never looked its real size. I believe Phil took it straight from the competition drawings and that there never was a careful restudy of the whole facade. I can't be sure about that, but I know McKim was never quite satisfied with the central motive, the main entrance, for shortly before I left the office* [in May 1900] *he told me to make a study of a new entrance. I did it very badly, I'm sorry to say.*[34]

The scheme adopted by McKim, Mead & White for The Brooklyn Institute of Arts and Sciences consisted of an enormous square, roughly 500 feet on each side (fig. 1.10). This square was divided into four quadrants by bisecting galleries nearly 92 feet wide. Where these galleries intersected, at the center of the square, was a circular memorial hall about 77 feet in diameter, capped by a dome rising nearly 140 feet from the floor. Around the periphery of the square were galleries about 40 feet wide, so that between the outer galleries and the crossed center arms were courts roughly 150 feet square. This basic scheme went back to such French models for museums as J.-N.-L. Durand's prototype of 1803.[35] McKim, Mead & White's principal innovation was to wrap the large quadrant courts with deep arcades and cover them with enormous glass skylights. The only element outside this square plan was a separate astronomical observatory at the southeast corner, where the diagonal of Washington Avenue made the building site wider.

The architecture throughout was severe Greco-Roman Classic, broad in scale, restrained in sculptural detail, and organized in the hierarchically arranged volumes McKim had learned at the Ecole des Beaux-Arts in Paris (fig. 1.11). In general, the facades resembled somewhat the Agriculture Building at the Chicago Columbian Exposition designed by McKim, Mead & White just the year before.[36] They were divided into emphasized corner pavilions, connecting wings, and bold projecting central pavilions. The prominent domed central pavilions had hexastyle Ionic-temple-front porticoes with the capitals patterned after those from the Temple of Apollo, Didyma.[37]

Three of the porticoes were to be approached by long dramatic flights of stairs, but in the original scheme the central pavilion on the eastern side had a circular portico integrated into a carriage drive, for this was the entrance to the public auditorium that filled the central arm on the east side of the plan. The corresponding central arm on the west side housed a large special exhibition hall rising through

37

1.9. McKim, Mead & White, perspective of competition entry for The Brooklyn Institute of Arts and Sciences. Line cut from Brooklyn *Eagle*, May 25, 1893.
1.10. McKim, Mead & White, plan of main floor, The Brooklyn Institute of Arts and Sciences, initial design including observatory.
1.11. Francis L. V. Hoppin, perspective of The Brooklyn Institute of Arts and Sciences, 1893, McKim, Mead & White, architects. Gouache and ink on paper, 24¾ x 65½ inches (62.9 x 166.4 cm) (The Brooklyn Museum).

three floors. The two central arms to the north and south contained three-story sculpture galleries fitted between flights of stairs that led to the upper galleries.

Above the basement level were three floors of galleries. These, together with the glass-covered courts, were to house collections arranged according to subject in the quadrants of the building. The two northerly courts were to house sculpture and architecture, both original specimens as well as plaster casts. In the galleries around these two courts were to be collections of industrial arts and natural-history exhibits from Egyptian and Chaldean times through the Gothic period. Just as the skylit southwest court housing the zoological exhibits was to be surrounded by galleries with engineering exhibits, so the southeast court was to house geological specimens encircled by galleries containing electrical and mathematical exhibits (the connecting link to the observatory was, appropriately, between the galleries for engineering and mathematics).[38] On the floor above the main floor were to be additional galleries and lecture halls, together with a restaurant on the west side, and on the third floor were more galleries for paintings and prints, a music room, and a reference library. Above these three floors of public space, atop the central arms and looking over the skylights of the courts, were additional floors of offices for administration and operation of the various departments making up the Institute, such as electricity, engineering, architecture, fine arts, music, and photography (fig. 1.12).[39] In total, over 1.5 million square feet of space were provided in the master plan.

One of the advantages of the McKim, Mead & White plan was its easy division into individual pavilions and wings, facilitating construction of the building in parts as funds became available and as the collections grew. During 1894 the plans were corrected and preparations made for building the first section. The master plan was divided into lettered sections (fig. 1.13), and in March 1894 the Trustees voted to begin building Sections A and B, the gallery wing

38

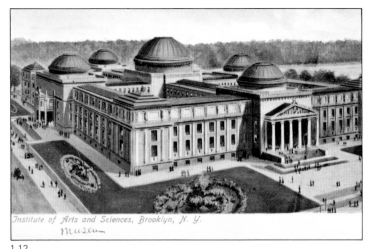

1.12

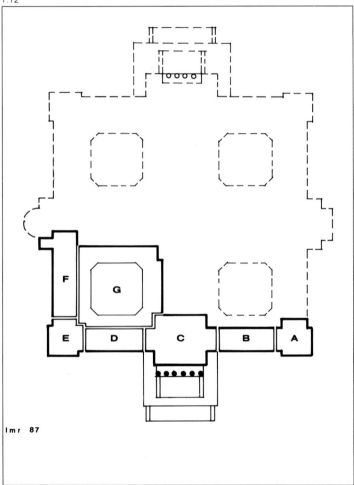

1.13

1.12. H. M. Pettit, The Brooklyn Institute of Arts and Sciences (proposed), circa 1904. Postcard (Courtesy of Phyllis Wrynn).
1.13. Diagram of The Brooklyn Institute of Arts and Sciences master plan indicating lettered sections (L. M. Roth).
1.14. The Brooklyn Institute of Arts and Sciences, view of West Wing (Sections A and B), dated June 2, 1897.

on the northwest corner. On September 14, 1895, ground was broken for construction by the P. J. Carlin construction company. For many of the details relating to the construction of this and subsequent sections, the office supervisor from McKim, Mead & White was Henry Bacon (later the architect of the Lincoln Memorial in Washington, D.C.). When this first portion of The Brooklyn Museum was completed in June 1897 (fig. 1.14), there was a festive opening ceremony.[40]

There were many problems that had to be solved as work commenced. One that surfaced early was how to provide for an auditorium, since in 1895 the prospects for building the principal auditorium in the west center arm were remote. The solution—whether it was proposed by Hooper or the architects is unclear—was to raise the level of the main floor by five feet, creating enough room to insert an auditorium in the basement level of the central pavilion.[41] Because of this, however, the principal entrance staircase had to be made much larger, leading to yet more problems that were to bring McKim, Mead & White's tenure as architects of the Institute to an end forty years later.

Among the many technical innovations included in the Museum was the new Frinck track or tube lighting in the paintings gallery. These slender tubes with electric bulbs were suspended from the ceiling, making little intrusion into the architectural space and yet providing light close to the paintings with no light bulbs exposed to the eye.

At the stroke of midnight on December 31, 1897, just months after the first section of the Museum opened, the city of Brooklyn ceased to exist as a political entity. As of January 1, 1898, after half a century of discussion and political maneuvering, Brooklyn became a part of the city of Greater New York.[42] Thus the building begun as a symbol for a proud, independent city now became simply another of many museums administered by the Parks Department of the City of New York. Gradually, the consolidation of the five boroughs had the regrettable effect of diminishing

1.14

the importance of The Brooklyn Institute.

Meanwhile, between 1899 and 1905, the City of New York built Section C of the Museum, the center pavilion, which included the magisterial staircase extending toward Eastern Parkway (figs. 1.15–1.17). Even before this was finished, in 1904, the city began construction of Sections D and E, the northeastern wing, a project that took three years (fig. 1.3). All the construction, including a temporary powerhouse built behind the Museum between 1902 and 1904, was again carried out by P. J. Carlin.

One of the most effective elements in eliciting public acclaim for the design, and no doubt helping to encourage continuing construction, was the handsome colored perspective of the competition design prepared in 1893 by Francis L. V. Hoppin (fig. 1.11), a skilled draftsman whom McKim entrusted in 1902 with creating perspectives of his plan for Washington, D.C. Hoppin's perspective clearly showed the kind of inscriptions to be cut in the frieze of the entablature   39

1.15

1.16

wrapped around the building. In focusing on the building's north side and in depicting the panel below the pediment on that side with the inscription MUSEUM OF ARTS AND SCIENCES . . . , Hoppin suggested that the principal entrance was to be on Eastern Parkway. In fact, the Grand Staircase leading down from Section C was never intended as the main entrance, for on the south side of the building was to be an even grander staircase leading to a broad esplanade extending out to Flatbush Avenue.[43] McKim, Mead & White prepared some studies for this grand southern approach, and the Trustees also engaged the Olmsted Brothers, who presented their proposal in January 1911 (fig. 1.18).[44]

As Hoppin's perspective showed well, the Museum building was to be graced by allegorical figures standing atop the columns of the walls and in the pediments of the center pavilions. As early as 1896, McKim, Mead & White had asked Daniel Chester French to design these allegorical sculptures, but nothing could be done until the sale of bonds had been approved to provide the funds, and that took almost ten years.[45] Beginning in 1904, Franklin Hooper, the Trustees, and the Institute's Executive Committee discussed what subjects were to be portrayed in the sculptures, following a scheme in which the Museum quadrants were to have Oriental, Classical, medieval-Renaissance, and modern themes in the names inscribed in the panels below the first-floor windows and in the sculpture at the attic level.[46] By January 1906 Hooper and the Trustees were ready to select a sculptor from a list of artists McKim, Mead & White submitted. Included were French, Augustus Saint-Gaudens, J. Q. A. Ward, Frederick MacMonnies, and Karl Bitter. At a meeting on January 26 the Trustees officially selected French as the principal designer of the monolithic 12½-foot attic figures and for the pediment groups.[47] During 1906, as the subjects for the allegorical figures were selected, French prepared a list of eleven assistant sculptors who would do the actual carving of the figures. The work was portioned out as follows: Herbert Adams—Greek philosophy, architecture,

1.15. The Brooklyn Institute of Arts and Sciences, center pavilion and Grand Staircase, circa 1914 (Courtesy of the Museum of the City of New York).

1.16. The Brooklyn Institute of Arts and Sciences, interior of main floor, circa 1914, displaying plaster model of master plan (Courtesy of the Museum of the City of New York).

1.17. The Brooklyn Institute of Arts and Sciences, interior of Rotunda, third floor (now fifth floor), circa 1914 (Courtesy of the Museum of the City of New York).

1.18

1.19

sculpture, and oratory; Karl Bitter—Chinese philosophy, religion, art, and law; George T. Brewster—Greek dramatic art and law; Kenyon Cox—Greek science; John Gelert—a Roman lawgiver, a Roman statesman, a Roman emperor, and a Roman orator; Charles Keck—Mohammed; Augustus Lukeman—Hebrew law, a Hebrew psalmist, a Hebrew prophet, and a Christian apostle; Edward C. Potter—Indian philosophy and religion; Edmund T. Quinn—Persian philosophy; Carl A. Heber—Roman epic poetry; and Janet Scudder—Japanese art (fig. 1.19).[48] The pediment for the Eastern Parkway portico was modeled by Adolph A. Weinman, following thematic material developed by French with McKim and Hooper (fig. 1.20). It depicts two seated figures representing Science and Art flanked on their right by figures representing Sculpture, Architecture (Egyptian in this instance), and Painting; to their left are figures representing Astronomy, Geology, and Biology.[49] During 1909 the figures were put in place.

Despite the rapid development of the Institute's collections, the urgency of building additional sections of the Museum diminished as other museums in New York required attention. In 1904, for instance, The Metropolitan Museum of Art commissioned McKim, Mead & White to prepare an extensive master plan providing for vast new gallery wings.[50] Even with the devoted leadership of Hooper, The Brooklyn Institute slipped ever lower on the list of New York City's priorities, and as early as 1904 Hooper was pressing for funds to have a complete plaster model of the Museum built as an incentive for continued construction. There was also a practical necessity for a revised master plan, for the only comprehensive drawings for the building were those done for the competition, and the nature of the Institute's collections had changed greatly since then. If future construction was to proceed smoothly, there had to be a set of drawings ready for use when required.

It took three years, however, to procure the funds for the model and master plan, and it was not until January 1907 that a contract with McKim, Mead & White was finally signed.[51] Two years later the revised plan and model were completed, and the model put on display in the Museum (figs. 1.16, 1.21–1.24). The principal alterations in the design involved the switching of the public auditorium and special exhibitions hall so that a new entry drive was incorporated on the west side of the Museum next to the reservoir property. The semicircular projection of the east center pavilion became simply a gallery. Externally the most visible change was a much taller center dome raised on a drum surrounded by a Corinthian colonnade and capped by a tall lantern (fig. 1.22).

1.20

1.18. The Brooklyn Institute of Arts and Sciences, plaster model, circa 1911, showing development of southern approach and Cherry Esplanade by Olmsted Brothers.
1.19. The Brooklyn Institute of Arts and Sciences, detail of northwest-corner pavilion with sculpture, circa 1915 (Courtesy of the Museum of the City of New York).

1.20. Daniel Chester French and Adolph A. Weinman, maquette of sculpture for north-entry pediment (Courtesy of the New-York Historical Society).

At the same time, McKim, Mead & White were instructed to prepare plans for the long-passed-over astronomical observatory. By October 1909 they had finished drawings for a straightforward rectangular building with three domes on a new site at the southwest corner of the building (fig. 1.25). But no appropriation was ever made for the $250,000 required to build this observatory or for the $28,000 needed to construct a more modest version designed by Teunis J. Van der Bent of McKim, Mead & White in 1930.[52]

After completing the new master plan and model in 1909, and following the deaths of White and then McKim, the firm of McKim, Mead & White did only minor work for the Institute. After 1910 McKim's chief assistant, William Mitchell Kendall, took charge of the project. Although the architects, the Director, and the Trustees began preparations for building Sections F and G in 1910, construction did not begin until 1913. This portion of the building, erected by contractors Wills & Marvin, comprised the gallery wing on

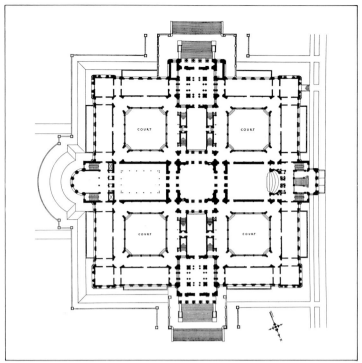

1.21

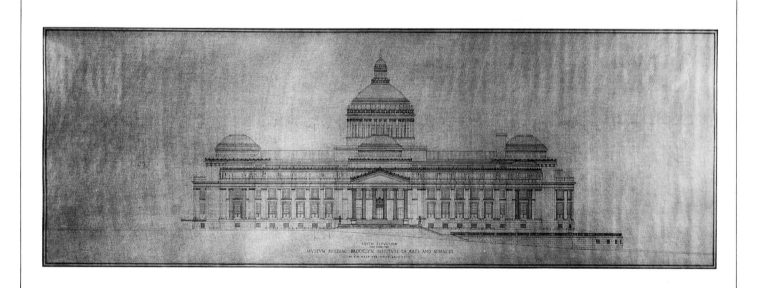

1.22

44

1.21. The Brooklyn Institute of Arts and Sciences, main floor of revised master plan, 1909. *Monograph of the Work of McKim, Mead & White* (New York: Architectural Book Publishing Co., 1915–20).

1.22. The Brooklyn Institute of Arts and Sciences, south elevation, proposed main entry, 1909. Ink on linen, circa 49 × 137 inches (125 × 348 cm) (Courtesy of the New-York Historical Society).

1.23. The Brooklyn Institute of Arts and Sciences, plaster model, 1909 (Courtesy of the Museum of the City of New York)

1.24. The Brooklyn Institute of Arts and Sciences, cross section of plaster model, 1909.

1.25. Elevation drawing of observatory, circa October 1909. Ink on linen, circa 23 x 36 inches (58 × 69 cm) (Courtesy of the New-York Historical Society).

1.23

1.24

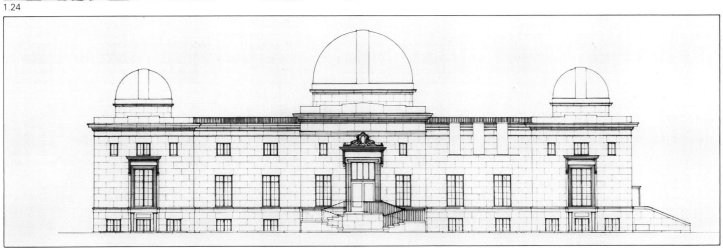

1.25

the northeast side and the skylit court of the northeast quadrant (fig. 1.26).[53] Construction was protracted, especially after 1914, in part owing to the impact of the First World War but also because in that year Franklin Hooper died, and thus the last great champion of the Museum building was gone. The wing and court of Sections F and G were physically enclosed by then, but the interiors remained unfinished until 1924–26, when this, the last major section built following the original designs by McKim, Mead & White, was at last completed and exhibits were installed (fig. 1.27).[54]

Meanwhile, the firm of McKim, Mead & White was appointed architect for the new Botanic Garden being created on the fifty-acre triangle southeast of the Museum. In 1913–16 they built the administration building and adjoining laboratory at the edge of the garden grounds next to Washington Avenue. In contrast to the imposing formality of the limestone Museum, the Botanic Garden headquarters building was based on Italian Renaissance garden casinos, with low, stepped massing and stucco construction.

Although William H. Fox, who succeeded Hooper as Director of the Institute in 1914, largely continued the programs Hooper initiated, the appointment of Fox's successor, Philip N. Youtz, as Acting Director of Museums in 1934 coincided with a series of sweeping changes. The number of constituent departments in the Institute was reduced, and some departments were closed altogether. Instead of being the flagship building of a multifaceted Brooklyn Institute of Arts and Sciences, the building on Eastern Parkway became a gallery of fine arts known simply as The Brooklyn Museum.

For two decades preventive maintenance on the Museum had been deferred. In particular, the front-entrance Grand Staircase had begun to show signs of age. Water had begun to penetrate through the stone paving slabs, weakening the reinforced concrete frame supporting the stairs. In 1926 Fox had asked McKim, Mead & White to prepare estimates of the cost of repair but work was put off; after 1930 fiscal retrenchment necessitated by the Depression forced continued postponement of repairs. The long delay and the worsening conditions prompted a letter of urgent concern from Frederick J. Adams of McKim, Mead & White to Director Fox in November 1933.[55]

There was also growing interest in providing easier and more direct entrance into the Museum. From 1930 to 1933 McKim, Mead & White prepared several schemes providing for a new entrance drive under the stairs, with vestibules at ground level and corridors that bypassed the auditorium. In 1934, at the insistence of Youtz, the architects also prepared a scheme with an additional entry that tunneled through the stairs at the level of the middle landing.[56]

How sad that such an honorable collaboration between architects, Director, and Trustees, born of the highest civic ideals and sweeping artistic vision, should now come to an ignominious end, strangled in a rising tide of acrimonious recrimination. Youtz, who was working with Civil Works Administration draftsmen on drawings of Mayan ruins for the Museum, began to develop a different scheme for the Museum entrance that called for the total elimination of the Grand Staircase and had his own draftsmen prepare drawings of his ideas. To McKim, Mead & White, such a drastic measure would have seriously impaired the integrity of their general design. They urged alternative solutions during January and February 1934 and refused to give their unqualified approval to drawings showing the removal of the stairs. To Youtz this refusal to follow his directives was tantamount to a breach of contract, and as the winter of 1934 warmed to spring the positions of both Youtz and McKim, Mead & White froze solid. Youtz wrote to the architects, accusing them of using ''obstructionist tactics,'' taunting them with the accusation that ''competent architects'' could have solved the problem of the entrance.[57] McKim, Mead & White appealed to Robert Moses, Commissioner of Parks, and Edward C. Blum, President of the Board of Trustees, for an impartial hearing.[58]

46

1.26. View of The Brooklyn Institute of Arts and Sciences and Eastern Parkway, showing completed building with Northeast Wing (Sections D, E, F, and G), circa 1915–25 (Courtesy of the New-York Historical Society).
1.27. The Brooklyn Museum, interior of northeast court (Section G), circa 1925.

1.26

1.27

Then, most curiously, in April 1934, while William Kendall of McKim, Mead & White was out of the country, his partner James Kellum Smith wrote Youtz that he had just seen a new perspective rendering of the proposed alterations to the Museum, minus steps, and wished to express his "relief and satisfaction that the change as shown upon this drawing has been accomplished with so much sympathy for the general design of the building."[59] With this apparent endorsement, Youtz's proposed changes were quickly approved by the Municipal Art Commission, and demolition of the steps began in a matter of days; by the time Kendall returned in June it was too late. To him, the building had been vandalized, and for a time he had attorney Carroll Blakely Low investigate whether legal action could be brought against the Institute.[60] The connection between McKim, Mead & White and The Brooklyn Museum came to an abrupt end. By August the first draft of a contract with architect William Lescaze was being prepared and a new era for the Museum was under way.[61]

To end the story in this way is to miss the important impact The Brooklyn Institute design had on later museum work by McKim, Mead & White. The early success of the Brooklyn project no doubt helped the firm win the contract to design large additions to The Metropolitan Museum of Art, additions that were carefully integrated with Richard Morris Hunt's grand pavilion on Fifth Avenue. And in 1911 the younger partners won the competition for the expansive Minneapolis Institute of Arts with a comprehensive plan that recalled that of The Brooklyn Museum.[62]

It should be noted, too, that in 1964 the hard angularities of the remodeled entrance were softened by the installation in front of the Museum of two large limestone figures of Manhattan and Brooklyn by Daniel Chester French. Removed from the entrance ramp of the Manhattan Bridge the year before during reconstruction of the bridge approaches, these proud figures provided a humanizing element at the entrance level, and together they formed a counterpoint to the figures at the attic story and pediment (fig. 1.28).[63]

An End and a Beginning

The Brooklyn Institute of Arts and Sciences as an academy-museum of all things for everyone was not to be; transformed (organizationally and physically) early in the twentieth century, it became The Brooklyn Museum devoted to the fine arts. An age characterized by cynicism might look back and wonder if Woodward and Hooper as patron and client, and McKim, Mead & White as architects, could truly have been so naive as to believe they could create an institute to be all things for all people. Although the creators of the Institute were romantics of a sort, they were also individuals of sincere conviction concerning public education, compelled to action by a driving sense of public mission. The question they put to themselves was how they could rise to the challenge of their time and of the promised greatness of Brooklyn and do anything less. Like McKim's colleague, architect Daniel Burnham, they knew there was no honor in making little plans. They aimed high, and now nearly a century later their aspiration has been rekindled in a call for a new design, couched in a new architectural language, to make The Brooklyn Museum no longer a fragment but a completed temple on the Brooklyn acropolis.

1.28

1.28. Daniel Chester French, figures of Brooklyn (foreground) and Manhattan (background), 1913–16, flanking entrance to The Brooklyn Museum. Originally designed for approach to the Manhattan Bridge, the figures were relocated in 1964.

48

Notes

1. General Jeremiah Johnson, quoted in Federal Writers' Project, *New York City Guide* (New York: Random House, 1939), p. 431. The character of pastoral Brooklyn from 1800 to 1860 is well illustrated in Linda S. Ferber, ed., *Brooklyn before the Bridge: American Paintings from The Long Island Historical Society*, exhibition catalogue (The Brooklyn Museum, 1982).

2. See John Kouwenhoven, "Brooklyn before the Bridge," in Ferber, ed., *Brooklyn before the Bridge*, p. 10; and Kenneth T. Jackson, *Crabgrass Frontier: The Suburbanization of the United States* (New York: Oxford University Press, 1985), pp. 27–30.

3. See Ira Rosenwaike, *Population History of New York City* (Syracuse, New York: Syracuse University Press, 1972), pp. 31, 36, 59.

4. For the development of the Prospect Park Plan, see M.M. Graff, *Central Park, Prospect Park: A New Perspective* (New York: Greensward Foundation, 1985).

5. Frederick Law Olmsted and Calvert Vaux, "Preliminary Report to the Commissioners for Laying Out a Park in Brooklyn . . . ," Brooklyn, 1866, reprinted in Albert Fein, ed., *Landscape into Cityscape: Frederick Law Olmsted's Plans for a Greater New York City* (Ithaca, New York: Cornell University Press, 1967), pp. 123–26.

6. Ibid., pp. 126–27.

7. Olmsted and Vaux, "Report of the Landscape Architects and Superintendents to the President of the Board of Commissioners of Prospect Park, Brooklyn," 1868, in Fein, *Landscape into Cityscape*, pp. 129–64.

8. For the political maneuvering leading to the consolidation of the five boroughs to form Greater New York, see David C. Hammack, *Power and Society: Greater New York at the Turn of the Century* (New York: Russell Sage Foundation, 1982), pp. 185–229.

9. Original purpose as described by Duncan Littlejohn in "Records of The Brooklyn Institute: 1823–73," quoted in Linda S. Ferber, "The First Hundred Years," in *Masterpieces of American Painting from The Brooklyn Museum* (The Brooklyn Museum, 1976), p. 2.

10. "An Act to Incorporate the Brooklyn Apprentices' Library Association," November 20, 1824, excerpt quoted in The Brooklyn Institute of Arts and Sciences, *Annual Report* for 1907, p. 85.

11. The building was sold to the city of Brooklyn in 1836 and was demolished in 1857 to make way for an armory.

12. "An Act to Extend the Charter of the Brooklyn Apprentices' Library, and for other purposes," excerpt printed in The Brooklyn Institute of Arts and Sciences, *Annual Report* for 1907, pp. 85–86. During the 1840s the Lyceum faded in importance so that by the end of the decade the Institute had taken over all the space in the Washington Street building.

13. John Blackburne Woodward (1835–1896) was a leading civic figure in Brooklyn, serving as president of the Brooklyn Art Association, the Brooklyn Department of Parks, and the Institute's Board of Trustees during the critical years when the new building by McKim, Mead & White was designed and begun. A statue by Brooklyn sculptor Frederick MacMonnies once stood in front of the Museum, honoring Woodward's dedicated leadership. A brief biography appears in *The National Cyclopedia of American Biography* (New York: James T. White Co., 1916), 15:47.

Franklin William Hooper (1851–1914) studied at Harvard University from 1872 to 1875, served on a scientific expedition in the Florida Keys, was principal of the Keene, New Hampshire, High School, and was then appointed professor of chemistry and geology at Adelphi College, Brooklyn, in 1880. In 1887 he was elected to the Board of Trustees of The Brooklyn Institute. For Hooper see biographical entries in *The National Cyclopedia of American Biography*, 13:46–47; and *Who Was Who in America, 1897–1942* (Chicago: A.N. Marquis Co., 1942), p. 585. See also the obituary in *The New York Times*, August 2, 1914, p. 15.

14. Rebecca Hooper Eastman, *The Story of The Brooklyn Institute of Arts and Sciences: 1824–1924* (The Brooklyn Institute of Arts and Sciences, 1924).

15. *The First Year Book of The Brooklyn Institute 1888–89* (The Brooklyn Institute, 1889), p. 46.

16. "An Act to Incorporate The Brooklyn Institute of Arts and Sciences . . . ," April 23, 1890, excerpt printed in The Brooklyn Institute of Arts and Sciences, *Annual Report* for 1907, pp. 91–92.

17. "An Act to reserve certain parts of Prospect Park . . . for art and science museums and libraries," June 5, 1889, excerpt reprinted in The Brooklyn Institute of Arts and Sciences, *Annual Report* for 1907, pp. 90–91. Prior to this the land had been scheduled for sale. This legislation stipulated that the land on which any educational buildings might be erected was to be leased by the city for a nominal fee; the 11.9 acres on which The Brooklyn Institute of Arts and Sciences was built was leased from the city for a term of one hundred years beginning in 1893 for the sum of a dollar per year. A copy of the lease indenture for the land on which the Museum sits, dated December 23, 1893, is in The Brooklyn Museum Library. The legislation also stipulated that any educational buildings erected on this reserved land "shall at all reasonable times be free, open and accessible to the public and private schools" of Brooklyn, as well as open and accessible to the general public "on such terms of admission as the . . . mayor and commissioners shall approve. . . ."

18. "Report Adopted by the Citizens' Committee on Museums, on the Scope and Purposes of the New Corporation . . . ," Brooklyn, February 1890, copy in The Brooklyn Museum Library.

19. This list of comparative institutions is cited in the article on Franklin W. Hooper in *The National Cyclopedia of American Biography*, op. cit.

20. For museum buildings as a type, see Nikolaus Pevsner, *A History of Building Types* (Princeton: Princeton University Press, 1976), pp. 131–35.

21. For art museums in the United States, see Helen Searing, *New American Art Museums* (New York: Whitney Museum of American Art, 1982).

22. The Brooklyn Museum is thus one of three major Beaux-Arts Classical museums begun in the early 1890s, including Shepley, Rutan & Coolidge's Art Institute of Chicago and Ernest Flagg's second Corcoran Gallery of Art in Washington, D.C.

23. *An Account of the Exercises at the Laying of the Corner Stone of the Museum Building of The Brooklyn Institute of Arts and Sciences . . . On*

Sunday Afternoon, December 14, 1895 (The Brooklyn Institute of Arts and Sciences, 1896), p. 10.

24. ''The Museum Movement,'' *The Ninth Year Book of The Brooklyn Institute of Arts and Sciences* (The Brooklyn Institute of Arts and Sciences, 1897), p. 280.

25. ''An Act to incorporate The Brooklyn Institute of Arts and Sciences . . . ,'' April 23, 1890, excerpt printed in The Brooklyn Institute of Arts and Sciences, *Annual Report* of 1907, pp. 91–92.

26. ''An Act to provide for the erection of museum buildings on park lands in the city of Brooklyn,'' excerpt reprinted in The Brooklyn Institute of Arts and Sciences, *Annual Report* of 1907, pp. 93–94.

27. The problems concerning architectural competitions at the turn of the century are discussed in Leland M. Roth, *McKim, Mead & White, Architects* (New York: Harper & Row, 1983), pp. 117, 182–83, 342–43.

28. The Trustees' requirement of the Classic style is reported in the Brooklyn *Eagle*, May 20, 1893, in an article giving the details of the jury's award of the competition. This and other clippings relating to The Brooklyn Museum competition are preserved in a Newspaper Clipping Scrapbook for 1892–94, McKim, Mead & White Archive, New-York Historical Society, pp. 183–86, 269.

29. Chronology and details of the competition provided by Minutes of the Board of Trustees, The Brooklyn Institute of Arts and Sciences, 5:100, 101, 109, 113, and The Brooklyn Institute of Arts and Sciences *Year Book*, 1892–93, pp. 95–98. A digest of correspondence between McKim, Mead & White and The Brooklyn Institute (prepared in 1938 by attorney Carroll B. Low) refers to a letter of October 26, 1892, from Franklin W. Hooper to McKim, Mead & White inviting them to participate in the competition (Correspondence Box 800–802, McKim, Mead & White Archive).

30. Although unsuccessful in this competition, William A. Boring (1859–1937), in partnership with Edward L. Tilton (1861–1933), later rose to prominence by winning the competition in 1897 for the Immigrant Station on Ellis Island.

31. Brooklyn *Eagle*, May 20, 1893.

32. Ibid., May 25, 1893.

33. For a discussion of the rise of the firm, see Roth, *McKim, Mead & White, Architects*.

34. Egerton Swartwout, ''An Architectural Decade,'' n.d. (circa 1930?), pp. 83–85. ''Garry'' was an office nickname for James M. Hewlett.

35. J.-N.-L. Durand's prototype is illustrated in Searing, *New American Art Museums*, pp. 14–15.

36. There was also a generic resemblance to the Fine Arts Pavilion at the Chicago fair by Charles B. Atwood; this, in turn, was based on Émile Bénard's winning design for the Prix de Rome in 1867 for an Exposition Palace for the Fine Arts. See Arthur Drexler, ed., *The Architecture of the Ecole des Beaux-Arts* (New York: The Museum of Modern Art, 1977), pp. 240–41, 470–75. McKim, Mead & White also designed several small art galleries, including the Walker Gallery at Bowdoin College, 1891–94, and The Pierpont Morgan Library in New York, 1902–7.

37. In a letter of May 18, 1896, Franklin W. Hooper thanked McKim, Mead & White for drawings of the capitals from the Hellenistic Ionic Temple of Apollo at Didyma and of the Propylaea at Eleusis that served as models for the capitals of the Museum (Box 182, McKim, Mead & White Archive, New-York Historical Society).

38. The nature and placement of the collections are indicated in the plan published in the Brooklyn *Eagle*, May 25, 1893, and in a slightly more detailed plan published in The Brooklyn Institute of Arts and Sciences, *Ninth Year Book*, 1897, p. 3.

39. The facilities on the second and third floors and above are noted in Buechner, *Handbook*, pp. 7–9.

40. Brooklyn *Citizen*, September 14, 1895; *Laying of the Corner Stone, . . . ,* passim. Henry Bacon's responsibility is evident in the extensive correspondence relating to development of the design, Box 182, McKim, Mead & White Archive, New-York Historical Society. Although the wing-and-pavilion organization of the McKim, Mead & White scheme facilitated construction in sections, it did not lend itself well to the installation of the rapidly expanding collections of the Institute.

41. The five-foot change in height is noted in Hooper to McKim, Mead & White, December 24, 1895, Box 182, McKim, Mead & White Archive, New-York Historical Society.

42. The vote for consolidation in 1894 was extremely close in Brooklyn and Kings County. Of the 129,211 valid ballots cast, 64,744 were for and 64,467 against—i.e., 50.107 percent for and 49.89 percent against—only 277 ballots difference. Hammack, *Power and Society*, p. 206.

43. In a letter to McKim, Mead & White, October 10, 1899, Franklin W. Hooper reminded them that the full name of the Institute was to be carved over the *southern* entrance, the principal entrance to the building; at the north entrance were to be carved the names of artists, scientists, and philosophers, as elsewhere on the building (Box 182, McKim, Mead & White Archive, New-York Historical Society).

44. Minutes of the Board of Trustees and Executive Committee, meeting of January 27, 1911, 11:633, The Brooklyn Museum Library. Olmsted Brothers was the name of the landscape architecture firm that continued the work of Frederick Law Olmsted after 1900.

45. The early decision to have Daniel Chester French design the sculpture is evident in numerous letters exchanged by Franklin W. Hooper and McKim, Mead & White, October to December 1896, Box 182, McKim, Mead & White Archive, New-York Historical Society.

46. Portion of the Report of the Director Relating to the Sculptures, n.d., bound into The Brooklyn Institute of Arts and Sciences, Board of Trustees and Executive Committee, *Minutes*, 9:651. In a letter, July (circa 6–13?) 1904, from Franklin W. Hooper to the Committee on the Museum Building, Hooper noted that ''it is Mr. Mead's judgement that the contract should be let to a first class sculptor without public advertising or letting, and that the sculptor French would be his preference to do the work. He states that Mr. McKim has had the matter of the pediment in charge; that he is now in Europe.'' Miscellaneous McKim, Mead & White Correspondence File, The Brooklyn Museum Library.

47. Data regarding the contract for the attic and pediment sculpture taken from The Brooklyn Institute of Arts and Sciences, Board of Trustees and

Executive Committee, *Minutes,* 9: passim. Because Daniel Chester French had long been working with the architects, his official appointment as supervising sculptor was something of a formality. In a letter to McKim, Mead & White, September 2, 1896, Franklin W. Hooper wrote that French had agreed "to take charge of the work of providing the sculptures for our building" (Box 182, McKim, Mead & White Archive, New-York Historical Society).

48. The responsibilities for the individual figures are noted in a copy of Daniel Chester French's account book for the Brooklyn Institute sculpture, The Brooklyn Museum Archives. Although French was responsible for the overall concept and design of the figures, the modeling of the individual figures was done by the various sculptors with whom French subcontracted and whom he paid. These individual sculptors provided half-size models (6′1″) to Attilio and Furio Piccirilli, who enlarged them to the final size.

49. See "The Institute's Sculptures," *The Bulletin of The Brooklyn Institute of Arts and Sciences* 1 (October 10, 1908), p. 84; and McKim, Mead & White, *Brooklyn Institute Scrapbook,* McKim, Mead & White Collection, Avery Library, Columbia University.

50. The Metropolitan master plan and extensions are discussed and illustrated in Roth, *McKim, Mead & White, Architects,* pp. 295–96.

51. The chronology regarding the revised master plan and plaster model is based on material in McKim, Mead & White, Miscellaneous Correspondence File, The Brooklyn Museum Archives.

52. Correspondence regarding the observatory projects, Box 37–42, McKim, Mead & White Correspondence, New-York Historical Society. Plans of 1909 are in Tube 2004 III, McKim, Mead & White Archive, New-York Historical Society.

53. It should be noted that particularly in Sections F and G, as well as in earlier sections of the Museum, McKim, Mead & White specified the use of a reinforced concrete frame and thus were among early architects to exploit this new technology.

54. Construction of Sections F and G was first discussed by the Trustees at their meeting of February 4, 1910 (Minutes of the Board of Trustees and Executive Committee, 11:460, The Brooklyn Museum Archives). The difficulties in completing Sections F and G prompted an attorney for the architects to comment that "the city of New York is most assuredly a difficult client with which to do business!" (Montgomery Hare to Burt Fenner, January 9, 1918, in Box 6, McKim, Mead & White Archive, New-York Historical Society).

55. Frederick J. Adams to William H. Fox, November 6, 1933, in McKim, Mead & White Miscellaneous Correspondence, June 1904–33, The Brooklyn Museum Library.

56. Sketches and detailed drawings of the proposed drive under the stairs, dated May 1929 through January 1934, are in Tubes 64, 65, and 66, McKim, Mead & White Archive, New-York Historical Society.

57. Philip N. Youtz to McKim, Mead & White, January 24, 1934, in Box 800–802, McKim, Mead & White Archive, New-York Historical Society.

58. Memorandum with copies to Robert Moses and Edward C. Blum, February 20, 1934, Box 800–802, McKim, Mead & White Archive, New-York Historical Society.

59. McKim, Mead & White ("JKS," James Kellum Smith) to Philip N. Youtz, April 27, 1934, Box 800–802, McKim, Mead & White Archive, New-York Historical Society.

60. Box 800–802 in the Correspondence Files, McKim, Mead & White Archive, New-York Historical Society, contains extensive correspondence between McKim, Mead & White and Carroll B. Low. Much of the material was numbered and a summary digest of the numbered items prepared, apparently as part of a legal brief. No legal action was instituted. Feelings within McKim, Mead & White and bitterness at the loss of control over their own design remained strong for several years, as is evident in a penciled comment next to a mounted unidentified newspaper clipping of April 14, 1938, noting the resignation of Philip N. Youtz as Director of The Brooklyn Museum in bold underlined letters: *Hallelujah* (located in the same correspondence box).

61. Details regarding the last phases of this exchange from Director's Correspondence file 1933–36, "McKim, Mead & White," The Brooklyn Museum Archives.

62. For discussion of these later museums, see Roth, *McKim, Mead & White, Architects,* pp. 295–97, 343.

63. See Michael Richman, *Daniel Chester French: An American Sculptor,* exhibition catalogue (New York: The Metropolitan Museum of Art, 1976), 143–50.

2. The Brooklyn Museum: Institution as Architecture, 1934–1986
Joan Darragh

Every wave of time superinduces its alluvion, every generation deposits its stratum upon the structure, every individual brings his own stone.

—Victor Hugo, *The Hunchback of Notre Dame*

Architecturally, The Brooklyn Museum represents a series of beginnings, a product of human enterprise on which every generation has laid its hands. Unfortunately, although each beginning has its value, the end result of all these beginnings—for all its symbolic celebration of change—is incomplete and qualitatively uneven. Since the Beaux-Arts vision of 1893 was abandoned with the termination of the McKim, Mead & White contract in 1934, the integrity of the original plan has been compromised by subsequent plans. Only recently, with the new beginning represented by The Brooklyn Museum Master Plan Competition of 1986, has an attempt been made to rekindle the fin-de-siècle flame and finally produce a completed building that will be true to the original architects' dream of a monumental symbol of civic and cultural pride.

Crucial to an understanding of how the architectural development of The Brooklyn Museum went awry over this half century is an understanding of the history of the Museum's Grand Staircase (fig. 2.1). Such entry stairs were a hallmark of the nineteenth-century Beaux-Arts formula to which the imposing building is stylistically bound. Indeed, as Robert Winter has recently written, no museum of the period "was without its grand staircase."[1] When first introduced in Karl-Friedrich Schinkel's Altes Museum, Berlin, of 1823–30, grand entry stairs signified honorific passage. As a photograph of visiting schoolteachers on the steps of The Brooklyn Museum in 1916 demonstrates (fig. 2.2), they were an architectural feature of great social importance. Today their significance is exemplified by The Metropolitan Museum of Art's stairs (fig. 2.3), which since their redesign by Kevin Roche have become so popular as a place for re-

2.1

2.2

53

2.3

2.1. McKim, Mead & White, The Brooklyn Institute of Arts and Sciences, central pavilion with Grand Staircase, north (front) elevation, circa 1910.
2.2. Teachers of Districts 33 and 35 on the steps of The Brooklyn Museum during sessions of the Teachers' Institute, September 11–21, 1916.
2.3. The Metropolitan Museum of Art, New York, Fifth Avenue facade, 1984 (Courtesy of The Metropolitan Museum of Art).

spite, performance, and social exchange that they have achieved their own cultural raison d'être. Even more important than serving this social function, The Brooklyn Museum's stairs helped orient visitors to the layout of the McKim, Mead & White plan. After mounting the steps, one entered the Museum at the Piano Nobile, the present third floor, passing into a great reception hall that McKim, Mead & White originally intended as the beginning of a ceremonial system ultimately leading through the building to four triple-height courts.

Today the arguments for having retained the Grand Staircase seem convincing. During the 1930s, however, they were swept away as the original lofty Beaux-Arts conception was replaced by a more populist-inspired, Modernist vision. In 1893 McKim, Mead & White and the Institute's Board of Trustees had responded to the call for a grand public gesture with a building whose Classicism implied high moral virtue, according to the tenets of the American Renaissance, and whose size and grandeur reflected the optimistic and expansive spirit of the times. The aesthetics of the 1890s, however, did not translate well to the sensibility of the 1930s. The American public had become more responsive to the egalitarian impulses associated with modern architecture, and in the context of the Depression the magnificence of the Beaux-Arts style seemed undemocratic and elitist.

Modernism as an architectural style first achieved widespread notice in America in 1932 as the result of The Museum of Modern Art's *International Exhibition of Modern Architecture*. Besides celebrating the work of Europeans such as Le Corbusier, Walter Gropius, J.J.P. Oud, and Ludwig Mies van der Rohe, this exhibition brought to public attention the American firm of Howe & Lescaze. Founded in 1929 by a Philadelphian, George Howe, and a Swiss, William Lescaze, the firm designed America's first major Modernist building, the new headquarters of the Philadelphia Saving Fund Society, of 1928–32. In 1930 Lescaze had de-

54

2.4. Howe & Lescaze, project for a museum of modern art in New York, scheme 4, 1930 (photograph of model courtesy of Lescaze Collection, Syracuse University).

signed several schemes for a new Museum of Modern Art building. His fourth scheme, later published in *Parnassus* as a prototype for a modern museum, consisted of a base with street-level entry, above which were stacked nine pavilions for gallery space (fig. 2.4). The composition, details, and program represented the most radical revamping of the subject in America, and in writing about the scheme Lescaze indicated his dissatisfaction with art museums of the past:

Most museums that we know are classic, monumental and, perhaps, imposing. A great flight of wide steps forebodingly leads to a great door foretelling a dimmed and hushed interior where life has been given its quietus into an inescapable morgue of dead art. Such buildings are neither inviting nor do they fulfill their purpose, and only the most audacious warily finds himself within of his own volition.[2]

While The Museum of Modern Art was increasing the public's awareness of Modernism and Lescaze was redefining the look of the American art museum, The Brooklyn Museum also experienced a change in direction: the appointment as Director in 1934 of Philip N. Youtz, AIA. Youtz, who had joined the Museum's staff in 1933, was the only architect ever to serve as the Museum's Director, and his six-year tenure was to mark a turning point in the Museum's building history.

Youtz had his own ideas about the proper look of a contemporary art museum. In a paper delivered before the Association of Art Museum Directors on May 10, 1936, he enunciated the architectural issues that informed his thinking, putting forth an eighteen-point ''Building Code for Museums'' that was to serve architects in designing museums of the future. According to Youtz, museums should have only one entrance—at street level—with doors small enough for a woman to open easily. ''Monumental stairs,'' he said, ''occupy an excessive amount of space and are dangerous in case of crowds. . . . Doors opening on a flight of exterior steps are extremely dangerous in case of a panic, for people are likely to fall and be trampled.'' Youtz further recommended that interior spaces be stripped of all ornament and called for ''banishing all such architectural stock and trade as niches, pilasters, cornices, monumental doorways, vaulted or coffered ceilings, etc.'' As far as colonnades, arcades, rotundas, and domes were concerned, they were ''sham architectural reconstructions and not real examples of classic design.''[3] With this rationale in mind, Youtz, inspired by Lescaze, pushed through a Modernist redesign of The Brooklyn Museum's central pavilion that included the removal of the Grand Staircase.

Youtz, who had been Curator of Exhibitions at the Philadelphia Museum of Art from 1931 to 1933, may have met Lescaze through mutual Philadelphia connections.[4] It is not surprising that he would have been a friend and champion of Lescaze, for they shared a passionate distaste for the Beaux-Arts style. Youtz was a relentless Modernist who deplored eclecticism and historicism, and Lescaze's work embodied the tenets of contemporary architecture. In commenting on the Howe & Lescaze Pennsylvania Saving Fund Society building, Youtz wrote: ''When the man on the street looks up to this skyscraper bank . . . he sees clean geometric surfaces, not the meaningless applied ornament dear to the Beaux-Arts tradition.''[5]

Youtz and Lescaze's Brooklyn collaboration began with the redesign of the Museum's entry. Structural and logistical problems with the staircase had become apparent soon after the completion of the East Wing in 1927. The main entry doors were large and heavy, and since the Museum is situated on one of the highest points in New York City there were substantial winter winds to contend with. By 1930 the stairs had been declared unsafe. A solution was urgently needed, for the Grand Staircase was the primary entrance into the Museum. The only grade-level entry, a small, side-level staff entrance, offered little accommodation to the one million persons who visited the Museum annually, and even 55

2.5

2.6

though the automobile had begun to play a significant role as a popular vehicle, parking lots or rear entries were not yet envisioned.

McKim, Mead & White had themselves alerted the Museum to the structural problems of the staircase.[6] Asked to resolve the problem, they submitted a redesign of the front entry in 1932 that included a vehicular drive passing under the stairs for a grade-level drop-off and entrance. Their design was consistent with the existing architecture and, according to the firm, satisfied the requirements of the institution by providing a secondary entry and structural upgrading of the stairs. But in 1933 Youtz requested that McKim, Mead & White submit an amended design that would include a cut-through entrance at street level after drawings he himself had sketched.[7] Given the diametrically opposed aesthetic sensibilities of architects and Director, design compromise was impossible. In time, when even more radical plans calling for the removal of the stairs were approved, the firm resigned.

Youtz had hoped—indeed worked—for this outcome. In fact, he would have hired Lescaze immediately to address the staircase and entry issue if McKim, Mead & White had not still been under contract with the City of New York as the architects for the Museum building. Instead he hired laid-off draftsmen from Lescaze's office[8] and submitted their drawings, executed under his direction, to McKim, Mead & White, who had agreed to sign them as their own in return for payment.[9] At the time of this dubious scheme, Youtz, who had already acknowledged his preference for Lescaze, lamented his having to continue to work with the architects of record, referring to them as "a slippery firm."[10]

Youtz's plans called for removing the stairs, creating an entry at grade level, and relandscaping the front of the Museum (figs. 2.5, 2.6); in addition, they provided for the conversion of the auditorium (fig. 2.7), then located below the entry level behind the stairs on the first and second floors, into the new lobby. Plans for this double-height, volumetric

2.7

57

2.5. The Brooklyn Museum, north (front) elevation, entrance stairs being removed, August 23, 1934.
2.6. View of The Brooklyn Museum during construction of new entrance on north (front) elevation and relandscaping of grounds, September 19, 1935.
2.7. McKim, Mead & White, The Brooklyn Museum, view of auditorium, first floor, 1919.

2.8

2.9

space were drawn by the draftsmen from Lescaze's office under Youtz's direction, and although Lescaze may not have had a direct hand in the lobby's design, he certainly was its godparent, for it is similar in feeling to the Howe & Lescaze Pennsylvania Saving Fund Society lobby (figs. 2.8, 2.9). It was intended to become not only a modern entry hall but also a space for the installation of art, as it is today. The new front entrance was designed as a modern two-story base to the original portico, with several doors opening directly onto a driveway at street level.[11]

Today the amputation of the ceremonial entry stairs in 1934 is perceived as insensitive and unfortunate (fig. 2.10). But to Youtz it was the beginning of a new age, one inspired by populist ideals. Although accessibility for the disabled was not then the consideration it is today, there was a concern with making the Museum available to the ''man on the street.'' In context, then, Youtz's zealous act was a thoughtful, progressive decision. A few years later, in 1939, the idea was taken a step further in Philip Goodwin and Edward Durell Stone's Museum of Modern Art, which featured a street-level department-store-style revolving door that scooped up passersby and shot them into the building. Other institutions similarly became involved with the issue of ''accessibility,'' as can be seen in Hugh Ferriss's rendering of a proposed grade-level entry for The Metropolitan Museum of Art in 1945 (fig. 2.11).

Once Youtz had successfully manipulated the design requirements that led to the resignation of McKim, Mead & White, he was finally able to hire Lescaze and pursue his dream of transforming a newer, more modern Brooklyn Museum into what he referred to as ''the style center of the world.'' In 1934 he commissioned Lescaze to design an overall plan to replace McKim, Mead & White's scheme.

Ironically, although Youtz's Modernist architecture clashed with the Museum's tradition, his rhetoric did not. The Brooklyn Museum, after all, had had a populist tradition since its founding as the Apprentices' Library in 1823. As

2.8. The Brooklyn Museum, entrance lobby shortly after completion, first floor, 1935.
2.9. Howe & Lescaze, Pennsylvania Saving Fund Society building, 1928–32, view of curved balconies adjacent to main banking room (Courtesy of Lescaze Collection, Syracuse University).

2.10. Parks Department, City of New York, rendering of plan for landscaping and improving The Brooklyn Museum, north (front) elevation, circa 1934.
2.11. Hugh Ferriss, rendering of proposal for removal of entry stairs, The Metropolitan Museum of Art, New York, 1945 (Courtesy of the Art Commission of the City of New York).

PARK · DEPARTMENT · PLAN · FOR · LANDSCAPING · AND · IMPROVING · THE · BROOKLYN · MVSEVM

2.10

2.11

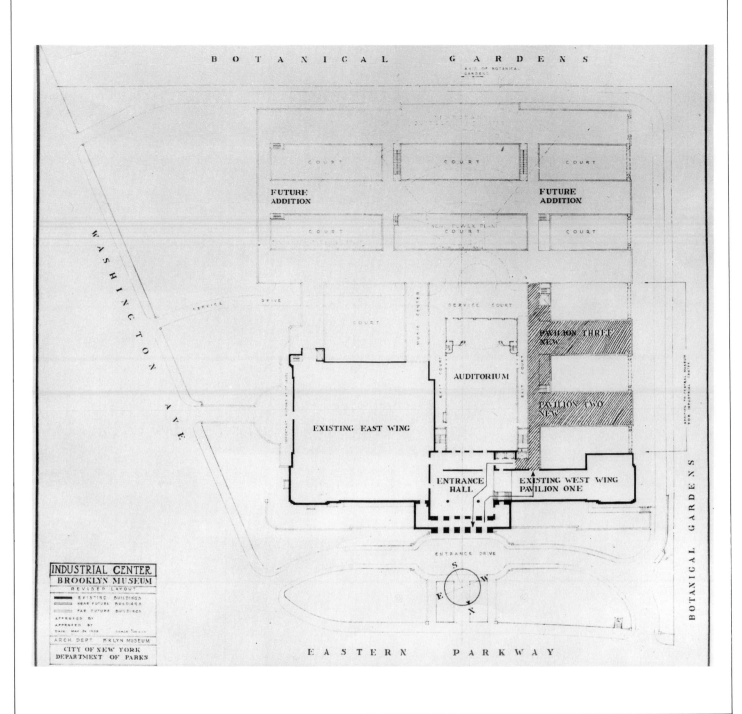

2.12

2.12. William Lescaze, plan of proposed Industrial Center, The Brooklyn Museum, May 26, 1935.
2.13. William Lescaze, west elevation and longitudinal section of proposed Industrial Center, The Brooklyn Museum, 1935.
2.14. William Lescaze, perspective of west elevation of proposed Industrial Center, The Brooklyn Museum, 1935, rendering by J.R. Petter.

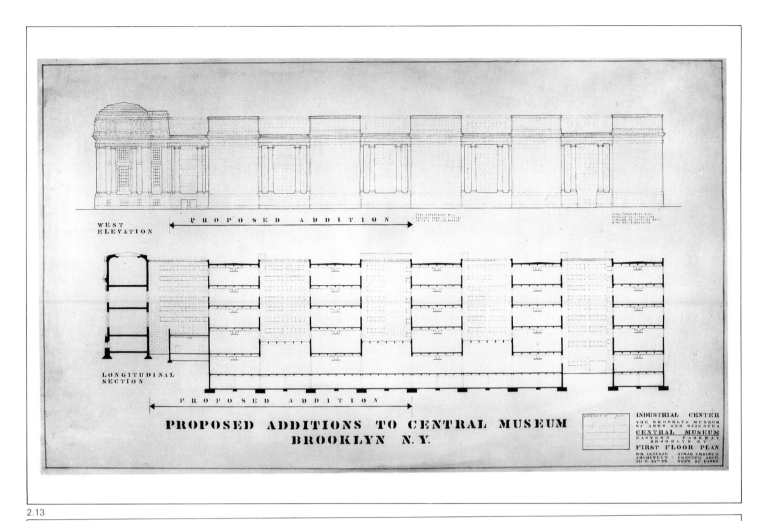

WEST
ELEVATION

PROPOSED ADDITION

LONGITUDINAL
SECTION

PROPOSED ADDITION

PROPOSED ADDITIONS TO CENTRAL MUSEUM
BROOKLYN N.Y.

INDUSTRIAL CENTER
THE BROOKLYN MUSEUM
OF ARTS AND SCIENCES
CENTRAL MUSEUM
EASTERN PARKWAY
BROOKLYN N.Y.
FIRST FLOOR PLAN
WM. LESCAZE   AYMAR EMBURY II
ARCHITECT   CONSTG ARCH
211 E. 48TH ST   DEPT OF PARKS

2.13

2.14

a department of The Brooklyn Institute of Arts and Sciences, it was committed to encouraging the study of arts and sciences "and their application to the practical wants of man" by means of "popular instruction." In the decade of the 1930s, Youtz continued this tradition by attempting to focus on industrial design as the art of the people. His goals were to broaden the understanding and appreciation of industrial civilization; to encourage higher industrial standards and achieve for the industrial arts the same recognition accorded the fine arts; to dignify the achievements of skilled industrial workers; and to educate the public about the role of the machine in industrial design.[12] He dreamed of exhibiting locomotives, airplanes, automobiles, and other "large modern wonders" as well as such smaller products of the industrial arts as refrigerators, furniture, and textiles—all in the context of fine art.[13]

Lescaze's plan for a Museum that would match Youtz's vision was announced in the August 21, 1935, Brooklyn edition of *The New York Times*. It included a 100,000-square-foot Industrial Center to complete the west elevation, a 2,500-seat auditorium behind the entrance hall lobby, and other unspecified additions located to the south of the existing building (figs. 2.12–2.14). Even though the full site was to be developed, there was no evidence of any attempt to make an aesthetic link with the Brooklyn Botanic Garden.[14]

Because the Industrial Center was the most immediate priority, its design was the most fully developed. It was to be located in the area south of the West Wing and to consist of a series of rectangular pavilions running parallel to the wing and perpendicular to the north-south axis. These pavilions were to alternate with open-air courts that would provide natural light. A continuous molding at the cornice line of the West Wing would link the pavilions by spanning the courtyards, and pairs of columns, reiterating those on McKim, Mead & White's west elevation, would complete the proscenium effect for each courtyard. Although the pavilions would have repeated the scale, massing, and material of the west elevation, as well as its tripartite composition (base, midsection, and attic), the result would have been decidedly mediocre, combining Modernism and Classicism to the advantage of neither by filling up the site with a prosaic repetition of undifferentiated blocks. Ultimately, Lescaze's plan and Youtz's dream were never realized, though they influenced subsequent alterations, especially to the interior.[15]

In architectural terms, Youtz's impact on The Brooklyn Museum would continue for decades. Attempts to replace the auditorium that was lost in his removal of the stairs, for example, would be central to the Museum's planning strategies for the next fifty years. Among the various spaces reorganized to compensate for this loss was the third-floor Renaissance Hall (fig. 2.16), which was renovated into a 300-seat lecture hall still used today as the only public lecture space in the building. In addition, as a "temporary measure," the triple-height Court of the Piano Nobile was transformed in 1935 into the Auditorium Court, which it has remained for the past fifty years (fig. 2.15). Modified by the installation of draperies, tapestries, and carpets to improve the acoustics, this space became popular for concerts (fig. 2.17), especially during the war years, when fund-raising programs such as "Music of Our Allies" drew audiences of up to 1,500.

Programmaticaly, Youtz's Modernism had an even more profound effect, for it brought about a greater focus on art. To that end, in the late 1930s the Museum deaccessioned its natural-history collections, freeing space in the West Wing, consolidating its art collections, and beginning its identity as The Brooklyn Museum as opposed to the Central Museum of The Brooklyn Institute of Arts and Sciences.

After all the natural-history collections were dispersed, the West Wing fifth-floor galleries underwent the first in a series of reductive revisions in which all ornamental elements of the Beaux-Arts composition were removed. Decorative baseboards, cornices, and the shouldered architrave trim of

2.15

2.16

2.17

63

2.15. The Brooklyn Museum, Court, third floor, 1985.
2.16. The Brooklyn Museum, Italian Renaissance Hall, third floor, 1932.
2.17. The Brooklyn Museum, Auditorium Court during concert, third floor, circa 1935.

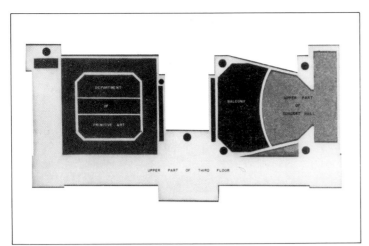

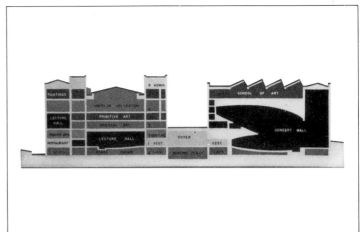

2.18

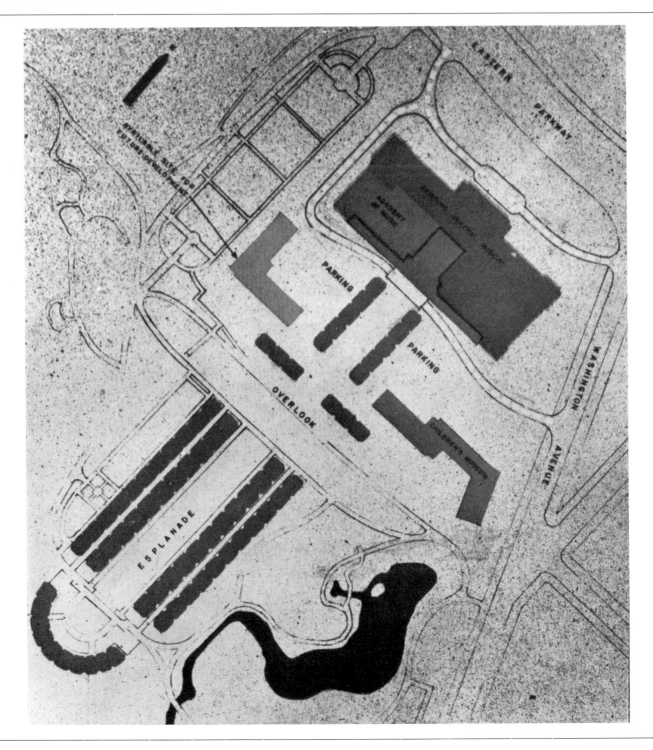

2.19

the doorways were replaced with streamlined versions. The terrazzo floors with their decorative mosaic borders were covered with cork, and the coved ceilings were simplified. This stripping away of ornamental interruptions, inspired by the naked halls of Bauhaus aesthetics, did little more than achieve an unadorned Classicism.

The deaccession of the natural-history collections also opened up 20,000 more square feet in the West Wing, and into this space in 1941 moved the Brooklyn Institute's Art School, which until that time had been housed in cramped quarters at the Brooklyn Academy of Music. In addition to enhancing the Museum's artistic and educational capabilities, the move breathed new life into the school itself. Although it would later fall victim to competing college art programs and have its remaining courses transferred to Pratt Institute in 1985, initially it thrived, attracting such teaching artists as Max Beckmann, Rufino Tamayo, Ben Shahn, and William Baziotes, and swelling with students under the G.I. Bill.

Besides the Art School, the Institute hoped eventually to bring all its departments together at the Museum site. Accordingly, in 1947 it hired the architectural firm of Brown, Lawford and Forbes to design a scheme for future development that would achieve just such a consolidation in capital improvements including renovation and expansion.[16] The Brown, Lawford plan, produced in 1950, would have balanced the massing of the East Wing by adding a 2,300-seat auditorium intended to house the relocated Academy of Music,[17] above which was to be an upper story meant to provide new skylit classrooms for the Art School (fig. 2.18). It would have completed the site by providing a separate building for the Brooklyn Children's Museum and, for the first time, a parking lot. In addition, it was the first plan since the original 1893 design to propose unifying the site aesthetically by continuing the north-south axis into the Botanic Garden (fig. 2.19). The interior double-height ceremonial spaces would have been divided by adding mezzanine

2.20

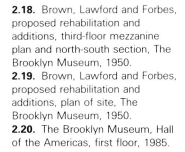

2.18. Brown, Lawford and Forbes, proposed rehabilitation and additions, third-floor mezzanine plan and north-south section, The Brooklyn Museum, 1950.
2.19. Brown, Lawford and Forbes, proposed rehabilitation and additions, plan of site, The Brooklyn Museum, 1950.
2.20. The Brooklyn Museum, Hall of the Americas, first floor, 1985.

65

2.21

2.22

66

2.23

levels: the first-floor Hall of the Americas (fig. 2.20) was to be transformed into a lecture hall, the third-floor Auditorium Court divided in order to provide two complete floors of gallery space, and the fifth-floor Rotunda surrounded by a sixth-floor gallery.

The plan, however, was too unwieldy in its desire to consolidate the Institute on one site. In both program and design it failed to provide an appropriate transition from the McKim, Mead & White plan, and in focus and intellectual rigor it fell short of Lescaze's 1935 plan. Fortunately, funding was held up in 1951 by a bill that provided construction funds only for civilian defense, and an attempt to get around the bill by having Parks Commissioner Robert Moses designate the new auditorium a bomb shelter failed.[18]

Still, although none of the major additions proposed in the plan was ever achieved, over a period of fifteen years a number of consequential interior renovations based on it were carried out. These staged interior rehabilitations began in 1952 with the renovation of the center pavilion, and the premiere space in this section, McKim, Mead & White's monumental Rotunda (see figs. 1.17, 2.21), underwent reconstruction in 1955 (fig. 2.22). The original Rotunda was to have been a culmination of the visitor's museum experience, with the Classical details and double-height space recalling the Piano Nobile lobby two floors below. The reconstruction, which included removing all decorative details, lowering the ceiling heights, and installing new lighting, produced a startling transformation (fig. 2.23).

As funding shortages continued to curtail the development of their plan, the architects of Brown, Lawford and Forbes were asked to come up with a new design that did not include the relocation of the Brooklyn Academy of Music. In 1955 they produced an asymmetrical pinwheel plan with a bridge connecting the Art School and the Education Division to the main building (figs. 2.24, 2.25). Although this effort recalled Walter Gropius's Bauhaus building of 1925, at best it was a banal reference to, rather than an understanding of,

2.21. The Brooklyn Museum, Rotunda, during the *Art of France and Belgium from the Panama-Pacific International Exposition*, fifth floor, 1918.
2.22. Brown, Lawford and Forbes, The Brooklyn Museum, west wall of Rotunda under reconstruction, fifth floor, 1955.
2.23. Brown, Lawford and Forbes, The Brooklyn Museum, Rotunda newly reconstructed as sculpture gallery, fifth floor, circa 1957.

2.24. Brown, Lawford and Forbes, The Brooklyn Museum, proposed plan and perspective of west elevation of Art School, Education Wing, 1955, as published in The Brooklyn Museum *Annual Report* (1955–1956).
2.25. Brown, Lawford and Forbes, The Brooklyn Museum, proposed Art School, Education Wing plan, rendering of wing by G.N. Lawford, 1955.

"MAKE NO LITTLE PLANS; THEY HAVE NO MAGIC TO STIR MEN'S BLOOD AND PROBABLY THEMSELVES WILL NOT BE REALIZED."

Daniel H. Burnham, Architect, relative to the Chicago Plan in 1907.

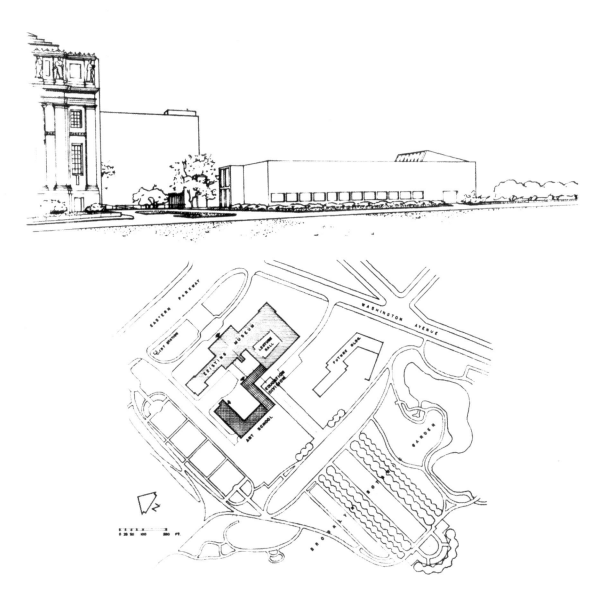

2.24

2.25

Gropius's elegant Modernist combination of form and dynamism. The published plan was headlined with Daniel Burnham's famous quote, "Make no little plans; they have no magic to stir men's blood and probably themselves will not be realized." But the plan that was being lauded as "no little plan" was little more than a reduced version of the 1950 plan and lacked the vision and inspiration of the Modernist ideal to which it alluded. Indeed it *was* a small plan, certainly far from magical. Futuristic visions, if only partly achieved, as in the original McKim, Mead & White plan, are not the products of economic hard times.

Despite the sincerity of both postwar plans it was not until 1967 that the parent body of The Brooklyn Museum, The Brooklyn Institute of Arts and Sciences, really began to address the Museum's long-range needs. In a special report by the long-range planning committee of the Board of Trustees, "New Departures for The Brooklyn Institute of Arts and Sciences," the Institute recognized the Museum's need for both more autonomy and more assistance, describing the alternative in stark terms: "For the Borough of Brooklyn there emerges a choice of heroic proportions— either a grand design, cost what it may, for physical, educational and artistic renewal or a backward step toward a cultural wasteland."[19] Included in the report was a plea for the City to participate in the Museum's revitalization.

The following year the City responded by allocating funds to install a complete climate-control system.[20] Since this installation would profoundly change the Museum's future, the Institute appointed a Board building committee to establish basic principles on which an architectural plan to accompany the installation could be developed. Of primary concern, of course, were the safety and well-being of the collections and the comfort of Museum visitors. But the committee also felt that any plan should encourage the development of educational programming and the expansion of the Museum's role as a cultural center of the Brooklyn community. Perhaps most significant was the committee's

stipulation that "The architectural integrity of this great McKim, Mead & White building—now designated a historic landmark—is to be maintained wherever possible."[21] It was the first time in nearly forty years that anyone considering the Museum's expansion had shown respect for the original architecture.

The building program that developed out of the committee's findings, however, was not nearly so respectful. Besides calling for the creation of new curatorial offices and the expansion of the Education Department, it proposed reconstructing the Auditorium Court, which was to receive a stepped floor for better visibility and appropriate equipment for improved acoustics. The climate-control equipment was to be housed across the south elevation along both the East and West Wings, finalizing the Museum's rear facade as an unceremonial service extension. Thus the same committee that had professed such rare sensitivity for the Museum's historic building proposed violating the one intact Beaux-Arts space and showed no feeling for the building's Garden elevation.

In the end the only tangible result of the committee's recommendations was the building of a scaled-down service extension designed by Prentice & Chan, Ohlhausen. Ironically, this extension, the only addition to the building since 1927, was produced during one of the hardest economic times in the Museum's and City's history. Although most City funds for climate control and construction were lost in 1975, an admirable strategy on the part of the Museum administration led to the acquisition of federal funds from the Department of Commerce in 1977, enabling the construction of the extension across the south elevation of the East Wing. Housed in the extension were a new boiler plant, Education Department offices, workrooms, and classrooms, curatorial offices, mechanical space, two new elevators, and space for a future auditorium and environmental-control equipment. Unfortunately, however, a reduction of the project budget by more than half allowed for nothing more

69

2.26. Prentice & Chan,
Ohlhausen, The Brooklyn
Museum, service extension of
south elevation, 1985.

than the amelioration of the Museum's programmatic needs via a mundane, Modernist wing (fig. 2.26).

Such an ad hoc approach to capital expansion provides short-term relief at best. In the long run it may cause headaches that the Museum will have to live with for many years. In an attempt to cure the Museum's circulation problems, for example, a new bank of public elevators for vertical circulation was installed in the service extension and a first-floor glass corridor was added along the west side of the East Wing from the elevators to the front entrance lobby (fig. 2.27). However, this solution confuses rather than rectifies the disruptive circulation flow that resulted from the unfinished McKim, Mead & White plan, for it leads visitors around rather than through the building, making their arrival on other floors an experience unrelated to the Museum proper.

By the time the service extension was completed in 1980, the Museum had been through nearly fifty years of abortive new beginnings, only to end up as a composite of disparate elements: the north, main Eastern Parkway facade had been denuded by the removal of the stairs (fig. 2.28); the west elevation, although romantic and nostalgic, had been left unfinished in the manner of a Hollywood set (fig. 2.29); the East Wing had received a Modernist slap on the back (fig. 2.30); and the south elevation, which Garden visitors view as they turn from the Cherry Esplanade overlook, had become an uninviting pastiche of the incomplete and the uninspired (fig. 2.31). The failure to formulate a strong master plan that would have avoided this outcome was the result of a number of factors, including Modernism's rejection of the Beaux-Arts ideal, the Museum's subordinate relationship to The Brooklyn Institute, and the troubled period in which the Museum sought to expand—one marked by the Depression and three wars.

Perhaps the difficult wedding of such a strong late nineteenth-century facade with a new design was a challenge that had to await the current willingness to re-evaluate the architecture of the past, the recent renaissance of the Borough of Brooklyn, and the Museum's own development into the singular, self-governing body it is today. At any rate the 1980s have brought us to a fresh understanding of the spirit that motivated The Brooklyn Museum's original architects, and, as we approach the turn of a new century, we are eager to follow Daniel Burnham's exhortation to make big plans.

2.27

2.27. Prentice & Chan, Ohlhausen, The Brooklyn Museum, corridor connecting service extension to front entrance, first floor, 1985.
2.28. The Brooklyn Museum, north elevation, 1985.
2.29. The Brooklyn Museum, west elevation from Osborne Terrace, Brooklyn Botanic Garden, 1985.
2.30. The Brooklyn Museum, east elevation and service extension of south elevation, 1985.
2.31. The Brooklyn Museum, south elevation, 1985.

2.28

2.29

2.30

71

2.31

Notes

1. Robert Winter, "Collection and Display: The Social History of Museum Space," *The Robert O. Anderson Building*, Los Angeles County Museum of Art, 1986, p. 27. For a complete discussion of the Beaux-Arts museum formula, see Helen Searing's summary of American museum architecture in her 1982 exhibition catalogue, *New American Art Museums*, for the Whitney Museum of American Art. Searing's exhibition and catalogue elicited a significant professional response that has raised the public consciousness with respect to museum building. See also Searing, "The Development of a Museum Typology," in Suzanne Stephens, ed. *Building the New Museum*, The Architectural League of New York, 1986; National Museums of Canada, *Planning Our Museums*, 1983; American Association of Museums, *Museums for a New Century*, 1984.

2. William Lescaze, "A Modern Housing for a Museum," *Parnassus* 9 (November 1937), p. 12.

3. Philip N. Youtz, AIA, "Museum Architecture." The Brooklyn Museum Archives.

4. The Brooklyn Museum Archives' Director's Files include numerous letters between Youtz and Lescaze documenting their friendship.

5. Philip N. Youtz, "Art and Industry," *American Magazine of Art* 27 (August 1934), pp. 434–35.

6. In 1930 McKim, Mead & White were commissioned to produce preliminary studies to alleviate reported unsafe conditions and deterioration of the steps.

7. Youtz's plan to add a cut-through to the already approved McKim, Mead & White stair design can be found in The Brooklyn Institute of Arts and Sciences exhibition file, no. 302, of the Art Commission of the City of New York and a rendered sketch, possibly in Youtz's own hand, in the McKim, Mead & White Archive at the New-York Historical Society.

8. In a letter to Lescaze dated December 20, 1933, Youtz vaguely outlined a drafting job involving the adaptation of McKim, Mead & White's latest submission regarding improvements to the Museum's front entry. The drawings had to be completed by January 8, 1934, and could not be signed by or acknowledged as the work of an architect, for the City was still under contract to McKim, Mead & White. However, Youtz wished to hire qualified draftsmen to work under his direction: "Our request is not for architectural services but simply for a drafting job. . . . Do you know any draftsmen who would be willing to do this work immediately?" Lescaze replied on January 2, 1934, "I have tried all along to find some employment for unemployed draughtsmen, and I shall be glad to take up the matter with two of them, whom otherwise I might have to let go." Plans were drawn and submitted to the Civil Works Administration on January 8, 1934.

9. An undated memorandum in the Director's Files in the Museum Archives indicates that Youtz had applied for a grant to pay McKim, Mead & White $2,000 to $5,000 for their signature on these drawings and had arranged to have them waive any right to future compensation for this design. Later correspondence indicates that Youtz rescinded this payment to the firm.

10. Letter from Philip N. Youtz to William Lescaze, January 23, 1934; letter from Youtz to John Hill Morgan, one of the Institute's attorneys, January 23, 1934; letter from Philip N. Youtz to Thomas A. Sully, one of the Institute's attorneys, January 29, 1934. The Brooklyn Museum Archives, Director's Files.

11. Some of the salvageable stone from the stairs was used in its facing. *The Brooklyn Museum Quarterly* 21 (April 1934), p. 47.

12. The Brooklyn *Eagle*, August 21, 1935.

13. New York *Evening Journal*, Brooklyn edition, August 21, 1935.

14. The plan departed from McKim, Mead & White's Beaux-Arts tradition not only stylistically but practically as well, for it identified several immediate phases and additional pavilions for future growth. The image published in the *Times* was this rendering of the west elevation. The issue of the completion of the west facade became critical to the 1986 jury (see Chapter 5 in this volume). During the 1930s the Garden continued to develop its site around the Museum as suitable in scale and feeling as a setting for the Museum.

15. Lescaze designed the Museum's Wilbour Library of Egyptology, 1933–34, which today houses one of the most respected libraries of Egyptology in the world. In addition to developing a plan for the Industrial Center, he also worked for four years, from 1934 to 1937, on a plan for the Institute's proposed Brooklyn Children's Museum, which was to be built on Brooklyn Avenue between St. Mark's Avenue and Prospect Place. The project terminated because of a lack of funds.

16. The Brooklyn Museum *Annual Report* for 1949–1950, pp. 19–25.

17. The downtown Brooklyn Academy of Music building that had housed the Academy and the Institute's School since 1908 was to be sold and the proceeds used to finance the new Museum building plans.

18. During this period the city-owned land and building came under the aegis of the New York City Department of Parks. Letters in the Museum Archives from December 22, 1950, to January 5, 1951, retell the bomb-shelter design funding strategy.

19. George D. Stoddard, "New Departures for the Brooklyn Institute of Arts and Sciences," 1967, referred to the report as "the first conscious attempt at long-range planning in our history."

20. Renovations to the existing building continued, and by the mid-sixties a much-needed art-storage unit was provided, and for the first time a parking lot was added. A few years later the City awarded the final contract for the installation of temperature and humidity controls.

21. The Brooklyn Museum *Annual Report* 10 (1968–1969), p. 35.

Part II. Competition

3. Professional Advisor's Report
Terrance R. Williams

In an architectural competition, the professional advisor is a member of the profession who is retained by and advises the client with the aim of ensuring equity for both the client and the architects. As Professional Advisor for The Brooklyn Museum Master Plan Competition, I served as the liaison between the sponsor and the competitors. In addition, my firm created the competition guidelines, building program, site plans, and base drawings from which the competitors worked. It was a unique and rewarding opportunity to work on a project of such ambition and vision and to follow a competition from its genesis to its resolution.

The Brooklyn Museum is an excellent example of American Beaux-Arts architecture that houses one of the world's premiere art collections. However, because the building was never completed as planned, its facilities are chronically short of exhibition, storage, and curatorial space. In recent years, the continuing economic growth of the borough has encouraged a wave of optimism that has engendered thoughts of finishing what was begun almost a century ago. This optimistic outlook, accompanied by new Museum leadership, inspired the Board of Trustees Building Committee to recommend the development of a much-needed master plan, and to select the architect of that plan by competition. In the committee's opinion, a competition was the most appropriate means of selecting an architect and producing a master plan with long-range goals to guide the Museum's development into the twenty-first century.

After the decision to embark on a competition the Board had to decide what kind of competition should be held and how it was to be run. Open competitions are appropriate for exploring the widest possible range of conceptual solutions to generic design problems. They are, by definition, open to all comers, students as well as professionals, and often involve more than one stage of design and submission—a process that can inordinately consume both time and resources.

The open competition also tends to remove the sponsor

3.1. Williams + Garretson. The Brooklyn Museum, existing conditions, 1986. Overall site plan (1″ = 100′) provided to the competitors.

3.1

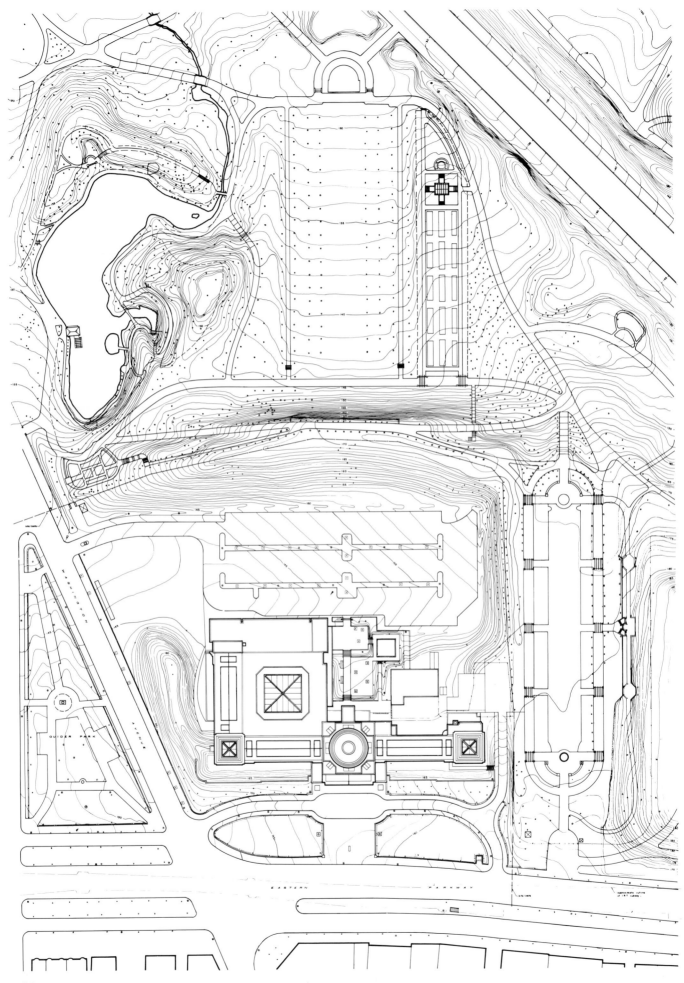

3.2

from the selection process: the Professional Advisor is selected, his or her guidelines are approved, and the findings of an independent jury are either accepted or rejected. This lack of sponsor participation and control, coupled with a primary focus on ideas rather than on professional qualifications, has relegated all too many open competition winning schemes to gathering dust in someone's archives.

Although invitational competitions offer the sponsors greater control of the process, they have been plagued by a number of abusive practices. The all-too-frequent use of this format to squeeze low-cost design services out of the architectural community has led to the irresponsible communication of sponsor requirements, to casual juries, and ultimately to serious misunderstandings and the creation of architectural camels that satisfy neither the expectations engendered by the original seductive images nor the sponsors' real needs. It was agreed that if a public institution such as The Brooklyn Museum was to select this format, every effort had to be made to make it *the* definitive invitational competition. To this end, the Board members established four goals: thorough documentation; equitable communication; responsible judgment; and, most importantly, control by the Board of Trustees.

One of the least understood factors in the creation of a successful work of architecture is the responsibility of the sponsors to the process. A work of architecture can only be as successful as the sponsors' charge to the architect is complete. Besides ensuring the accuracy of the architectural design, careful preparation by the sponsors permits them to educate themselves as to their needs *prior* to the selection of an architect.

In the case of The Brooklyn Museum, this necessary preparation had particular significance. First, it meant that the master-plan process commenced with an assessment of actual needs *without design prejudice*. Secondly, program preparation and data collection became an important vehicle for including staff and pertinent City agencies in formulating

the institution's future. Programming began with a detailed assessment of the collections. What were their storage requirements? What were the staffing and curatorial requirements? Were there any required adjacencies, or simply preferred ones? Like ripples in a pool, programming worked outward from collections to support services, administration, and security. The final result was not simply a building program; it was also a means of assessing the total reorganization of the institution and how it functioned. The program became a vehicle for engaging and educating the Trustees and staff. During the preparation of the building program a number of design constants and considerations that must be present in any architectural scheme for the Museum were identified. These included the return of the third floor as the Piano Nobile and the principal point of entry; specific uses for some spaces and suggested ones for others; the completion of the McKim, Mead & White link with the Brooklyn Botanic Garden; and the examination of urban design opportunities, including an investigation of adjacent park areas that could be made part of a revitalized urban design strategy for the Museum's immediate surroundings (fig 3.1).

There were a number of other factors that also contributed greatly to the success of the competition. First, a complete data base was prepared to enable the competitors to begin designing on day one. The data base included up-to-date building plans, sections, and elevations (fig. 3.2); site plans including topography and all pertinent site data; and program diagrams to scale. Much of this information had to be retrieved from various City repositories of public building records. All competitors received a competition package that included base drawings printed on reproducible and washable Mylar. Without this package, which took a year of researching, collating, and drafting to produce, it would have been impossible to hold a successful competition.

By furnishing such a complete data base, we were able to limit the competition time span to two and a half months   79

3.2. Williams + Garretson. The Brooklyn Museum, existing conditions, 1986. Technical site plan (1″=40′) provided to the competitors.

in order to focus the competitors' time on design rather than preparation and to protect them from their own architectural zeal. The demand on competitors' resources was extensive enough to warrant an increase in compensation beyond the then-established norm of $25,000. The Board voted unanimously to increase the honorarium to $50,000.

The preparation of the documentation coincided with the beginning of the selection process. In keeping with the Board's desire to govern throughout, it retained the largest block of seats (four) on the ten-member selection committee. The other six seats were occupied by two senior staff members, three City officials, and one architectural critic.

The process began with a review of five years of international architectural publications to determine who was doing what and where. This exercise led to the establishment of several unique and essential criteria. For instance, it became apparent that a large practice or previous museum experience were no guarantee of design excellence. What was demonstrably important, however, was the architect's ability to handle design complexity with contextual sensitivity. These observations influenced the structuring of the ''Request for Qualifications'' (RFQ) to ensure that the competition would not be financially onerous or that older, larger firms could not simply overpower the presentations of younger, smaller candidates. We requested a strict format with specific areas of information. These included project management, work load of the firm, Federal Government Standard 254 and 255 forms (with blank forms forwarded to overseas candidates), references (all of whom were contacted during the semifinal round), and no more than fifteen plates illustrating a total of five projects.

One hundred three firms worldwide received the RFQ. Of the fifty-seven that responded, thirty became serious contenders. After considerable debate, ten semifinalists were invited for interviews, and five finalists were ultimately selected. The selection committee's role was perhaps the most important one in the entire process. The committee rejected both a conservative, predictable slate and an equally inappropriate one of boutique firms on the cutting edge of design fashion. Instead, it stuck by its criteria and selected a well-balanced mix of talent, size, and point of view.

One of the most common abuses in invitational competitions is the careless and uneven distribution of information. In the case of The Brooklyn Museum, every effort was made to ensure that all parties received the same information at the same time. Given the volume and complexity of material to be disseminated, this was no easy task. It was accomplished with a comprehensive three-day briefing session and strict control of all communications (figs. 3.3–3.5). Any violation of the communication rules would have led to the immediate disqualification of the team involved and forfeiture of half the honorarium.

Over the summer of 1986, while the competitors were hard at work, so was the Museum's staff. One of the original McKim, Mead & White galleries on the fourth floor was selected as the Competition Jury Gallery. This area, which had been previously occupied by the former Art School and was slated for phase-one construction, became the perfect place for the Jury to review the Museum's programmatic future. The Brooklyn Museum crew cleaned, polished, and painted this transitional area until a truly elegant space emerged ready and waiting for the entries to arrive.

The competitors were required to submit a total of twelve boards, a model, and multiple sets of technical drawings and reports. The reports included detailed information concerning conformance to program, phasing, and costs of the project, as well as a written description of the scheme. Obviously, the quantity and depth of material to be reviewed were more than a jury could possibly deal with. This factor, coupled with the Museum's desire to involve pertinent City agencies in all phases of the competition, led to the formation of the Technical Review Panel. This panel was composed of four Museum staff members, two representatives from City government, one representative from the Brooklyn Bo-

3.3. Architects' tour, June 25, 1986. Joan Darragh, Vice Director for Planning, and Terrance Williams, Professional Advisor, introduce the competitors to the guidelines and building program.
3.4. Architects' tour, June 25, 1986. Representatives from the competing firms.
3.5. Peter Casler, Director of Capital Planning and Construction, Brooklyn Botanic Garden, leads architects through the Garden, June 25, 1986.

3.6. The Brooklyn Museum, West Wing, fourth floor, showing architectural boards and models in place for Jury viewing. Lots were drawn for placement of submissions.

3.3

3.4

3.5

tanic Garden, and two consultants to assist in engineering, construction, and cost assessment. Once the sixty boards, six models (including one of McKim, Mead & White's original design), twenty existing-condition drawings and program diagrams, and copies of McKim, Mead & White's original drawings were installed, the panel convened for the judgment process (fig. 3.6). The panel was charged with the responsibility of assessing and reporting to the Jury the degree of conformance or variance with the building program, design guidelines, and local codes. It was also required to check the veracity of construction costs and feasibility of the proposed phasing. In preparing summaries for the Jury, the panel covered a tremendous amount of ground and freed the Jury from dozens of hours of tedious, but essential, review.

Although Jury Chairman Klaus Herdeg covers the workings of the Jury admirably in another chapter, one or two comments are appropriate here. First, its composition. Once the Board had decided that this was to be a "hands on" process, it was essential that it maintain control throughout. The degree of Museum representation on all decision-making (and advisory) bodies reflected this policy. The Board and staff were represented on the Jury by Chairman Alastair B. Martin, President Robert S. Rubin, Building Committee   81

3.6

3.7

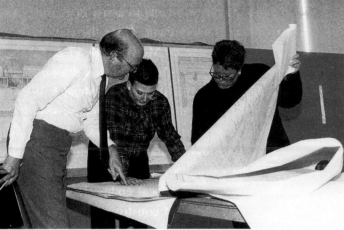

3.8

3.9

Chairman Jeffrey C. Keil, and Director Robert T. Buck. The three outside professionals were Jury Chairman Klaus Herdeg from Columbia University and architects Phyllis Lambert of Montreal and James Stirling of London (figs. 3.7, 3.8). In a worst-case scenario, then, the Museum could theoretically maintain a majority position. Fortunately, the real deliberations ended in unanimous accord.

Another point that should be made about the Jury is the importance of having an educator of Herdeg's stature as Chair. Architects dealing with their own discipline have an obvious advantage and often intimidate laymen even when not intending to do so. It was our belief that an architect who was an experienced educator as well would be a key player and might help to bridge this gap between professional and layman. We were right. Herdeg's ability to explain some of the more arcane professional issues to the others proved invaluable and had much to do with the ultimate enthusiastic unanimity (fig. 3.9).

The Jury's deliberations were a fitting climax to a long and thoughtful process, one that permitted the sponsors to prepare themselves in advance and afforded them the opportunity to see how five leading architects would apply their talents to resolving the Museum's specific problems. The diligence of the predesign work contributed significantly to the production of five useful schemes, not simply seductive, superficial images. This preparation is a factor that will ultimately shave time and money from the design and construction process.

As a result of conducting this competition the Museum benefited from the opportunity to review five complete proposals for a master plan while engaging its Board and Director in an informative process. The final outcome was more than merely the selection of the right architect for the job; the Museum became a most enlightened client in the process.

3.7. Jeffrey C. Keil, Trustee and Building Committee Chairman, viewing model by Skidmore, Owings & Merrill during the meeting of the Jury.
3.8. Robert T. Buck, Director of The Brooklyn Museum, Phyllis Lambert, architect, and Joan Darragh, Vice Director for Planning of The Brooklyn Museum, viewing architectural plans during meeting of the Jury.
3.9. Klaus Herdeg, Jury Chairman, addressing the Jury, October 7, 1986.

4. Finalists

**Atkin, Voith & Associates with
Rothzeid Kaiserman Thomson & Bee**

Team
Tony Atkin
Daniela Holt Voith
Michael Pearson
Charles Evers
David Genther
Lisa Hopkins
Shep Houston
Nicholas Iselin
Cameron Mactavish
David Mayernik
Mary Nixon
Samuel Olshin

Margaret Goldner
  Rabinowitz
Simon Tickell
Partnership Team
Bernard Rothzeid
Carl Kaiserman
Carmi Bee
Daniel Silver
Scott Groom
Sandra Halvorsen
Luis Salazar
Martin Tuzman
Watercolor Renderings
Cameron Mactavish

41

Tony Atkin
Charles Evers
David Genther
David Mayernik
Mary Nixon
Samuel Olshin
Michael Pearson
Simon Tickell
Presentation Model
Laura Martin Kass
Mark Webber
Cost Estimators
Charles Arena, Arena and
Company

Structural Engineers
Thomas Leidigh, Keast and
Hood Company
Landscape Architects
Anthony Walmsley and
Patricia O'Donnell,
Walmsley and Company
Restoration
David Hollenberg, John
Milner and Associates
Security and Fire
Joseph M. Chapman and
Robert Ducibella, Joseph
M. Chapman, Inc.

Lighting Designer
George Izenour

Daniela Holt Voith and Tony Atkin

Atkin, Voith & Associates, a fourteen-person Philadelphia architecture and design firm, was founded in 1979 by Tony Atkin. The firm was reorganized in 1985 when Daniela Holt Voith joined in its ownership. Over the last eight years the firm has grown rapidly in size and in the diversity of its projects. Atkin, Voith & Associates' design specialty derives from the principals' belief in the expressive power of architectural image and in the evolution of traditional forms through necessary innovation. Like early twentieth-century architects, they aspire to a broad eclecticism, selecting an appropriate idiom for each project to achieve practicality, beauty, and individuality. Atkin, Voith & Associates has received a number of design awards, including citations from *Progressive Architecture* and the Philadelphia Chapter of the American Institute of Architects.

The principal project designer for The Brooklyn Museum Master Plan Competition was Tony Atkin, AIA. Atkin, born in 1950, studied at the University of Utah before receiving a master of architecture degree at the University of Pennsylvania. After graduating, he worked as design draftsman and architect for Venturi, Rauch and Scott Brown and later as a historic researcher and architect for John Milner Associates. Currently, Atkin teaches architectural design at the University of Pennsylvania. He has been a visiting lecturer and critic at many of the country's leading architecture schools.

Daniela Holt Voith was the coordinating designer for the competition. She was also in charge of program compliance and the writing and production of the technical report. Voith, born in Philadelphia in 1954, studied architectural history at Bryn Mawr College before receiving her master of architecture degree from Yale University. She teaches architectural design at Bryn Mawr College and has been a guest critic and lecturer on architectural history and design.

Rothzeid Kaiserman Thomson & Bee, partner in the joint venture, strongly supplemented Atkin, Voith & Associates with its technical skill, ability to coordinate and produce documents for large-scale projects, familiarity with New York City, and experience with sensitive and sophisticated renovation and restoration. For the competition, the firm was responsible for construction-phasing projections, cost estimates, specifications, zoning compliance, and comparative square footages. Rothzeid Kaiserman Thomson & Bee, originally formed in 1963, is a forty-member firm whose practice has focused on the restoration and renovation of existing buildings. The firm has received the American Institute of Architects National Award for Excellence as well as awards from *Builders* and *Interiors* magazines.

Bernard Rothzeid, FAIA, founding principal of the firm, received his master's degree in architecture from the Massachusetts Institute of Technology and is currently chairman of the Landmarks Committee for the New York City chapter of the American Institute of Architects.

Carl Kaiserman, AIA, is Principal in Charge of the production of contract documents and field observation. Kaiserman received his bachelor of architecture degree from the City University of New York.

Carmi Bee, AIA, Principal in Charge of Design for the firm, received his master's degree in architecture from Princeton University.

Project Description

Our design for The Brooklyn Museum master plan stems from the imperatives of the original McKim, Mead & White competition scheme, the Brooklyn Botanic Garden, and the programmatic directive to combine the two. The Botanic Garden's Cherry Esplanade and Osborne Terrace, the existing Museum building, and the large earth berms on the Museum's grounds were built as part of a total vision. Now, lying in wait, they remain incomplete. By emphasizing the major axes, acknowledging and reinterpreting the footprint of the original four-courtyard plan, and using a strong and sympathetic architectural vocabulary, our design unites the pieces while making a modern, functional museum.

The reconstructed front stair and double-height entry hall of our plan will reestablish the third floor as the Piano Nobile and return the north front to its original significance and grandeur. The new south front, with its colonnades, terraces, stairs, and large hemicycle, faces and completes the Botanic Garden elevation. The south entrance lobby, which opens to the second floor, is capped by a gently arched handkerchief dome and complements its northern counterpart.

The large central hall is a single legible space that connects the two lobbies and reinforces the axis that runs from Eastern Parkway, through the Museum and the Botanic Garden, to the reflecting pool at the end of the esplanade. This Great Hall rises three stories to a vaulted, coffered ceiling. Sunlight washes the hall's balconies and punctuates its crossings. All the gallery floors, stairs, escalators, and elevators are organized along this powerful north-south axis.

We designed a sequence of water elements as a subtle accompaniment to this axial progression. It starts with a pair of dish-shaped fountains in the Great Hall. A long, rectangular reflecting pool in the south lawn points to the newly developed Botanic Garden overlook and its stepping cascades, which culminate in a pool at the end of the esplanade.

From this pool, turning back north, the visitor will have a vista dominated by the calm new south front.

Originally, the Museum was conceived as a Classical object set on a crisply defined and substantial pedestal base. By removing the existing trees from the Museum front and continuing the base around the entire Museum, the original relationship of the Museum and park has been restored. We have reaffirmed the validity of the romantic landscape as the setting for the formal, Classically inspired cultural institution.

Organization of the Galleries. Architecturally, the galleries are organized around the new Great Hall and four major volumes that echo the McKim, Mead & White plan. Because the public will enter on the Piano Nobile and the first floor (for groups and nighttime activity), the existing second level of the Museum was developed as a main gallery floor. Two twenty-five-foot-high, one-hundred-foot-long galleries rise through the third floor in the locations of the southern courts of the turn-of-the-century plan. Visual connection to the monumental galleries, one for special exhibitions, the other for contemporary art, is made from the Piano Nobile from two long cross-axial balconies. These end in broad stairs that descend to the second level.

The Beaux-Arts Court, the only existing of four originally planned courts, will be faithfully restored. The northwest quadrant has been given an exterior garden court which will house the architectural fragments and give views of the Osborne Terrace. The galleries on the north are organized in linear progressions around these two main spaces, forming large loops.

The plan gives the Museum visitor's experience primary emphasis. Because the galleries are organized in loops and the quadrants of the Museum are clear, we have given each collection a memorable location. Intense concentration is encouraged in well-proportioned and well-lit galleries. Between collections, areas along the major axes have been specifically designed for rest and contemplation. Thus, the galleries have been given sequence and cadence.

Disposition of the Collections. We have designed the galleries to provide the Museum with a variety of flexible spaces. There are galleries with and without natural light; high-ceilinged and moderate-height galleries; large, open-spaced galleries in addition to more intimately scaled spaces; galleries for permanent installations; and galleries that can be easily adapted to many purposes.

As part of the planning process, we have paid close attention to the disposition of the Museum's collections. In placing them, we have given each collection a clearly definable location. The placement of the collections in relation to one another was a complicated process, as the existing building seemed to dictate certain gallery placements that did not always coincide with the programmatic directives.

As we saw it, these were the givens:
1. The Beaux-Arts Court should house the Beaux-Arts collection.
2. Since most of the period rooms had been recently reinstalled, the Decorative Arts collection should remain on the fourth floor.
3. Because the Museum wishes to use the restored McKim, Mead & White galleries for display, collections that can tolerate natural light should be located in these galleries.

Further, there seemed to be three ways of relating the diverse collections to one another: chronologically, geographically, and by artistic tradition. The overlapping of these three rationales produced the disposition of the collections within our design.

89

1. Chronologically: The sequence begins on the Piano Nobile with the Egyptian collection, which contains the oldest objects in the Western tradition.
2. Geographically: The major world units have been kept together.
3. By tradition: The Western tradition, starting with the Egyptian, is carried up through the Museum (Decorative Arts and Costumes and Textiles on the fourth floor; American and European Painting and Sculpture on the fourth and fifth floors). The non-Western collections (Spanish Colonial American, New World, African, and Oceanic Art; Egyptian, Classical, and Ancient Middle Eastern Art; Oriental and Islamic Art) are located on the second floor. The Western and non-Western collections physically meet at the Contemporary Arts and Special Exhibition galleries.

Two pavilions on the south facade contain objects that represent the organization of the galleries and the strengths of the Museum's collections: one houses the Auguste Rodin bronzes, the other the Northwest American Indian totem poles.

Organization of the Nonpublic Museum. The conflicting but necessary goals of the safety and accessibility of the collection were of prime importance to the configuration of our scheme. The legible organization of the gallery spaces and a logical sequence for the collections within the Museum are the most visible aspects of museum design but satisfy only about a third of the Museum's requirements. The storage and preservation of the collection is one of the Museum's primary objectives. The unusual vertical configuration of the existing Museum block and the existence of the Prentice & Chan, Ohlhausen addition led us to the concept of a vertical storage tower. With some modification, the Prentice & Chan, Ohlhausen addition becomes a nine-level storage tower that vertically connects the art shipping and receiving functions on the basement level with the collection-man-

90

agement, curatorial, and administrative functions on the top levels of the Museum. The tower is organized so that the storage of the collections occurs, as much as possible, on the same level with corresponding display areas. We have minimized the horizontal movement of the objects (which presents the greatest threat to their conservation) through this device.

By locating collection management, curatorial offices, and administration on the top levels of the Museum, we have provided high-quality work space with light and spectacular views. The public reception area for this management "triumvirate" is on the sixth floor and is accessible by the south elevators. A pair of staff elevators connects the staff parking directly with these offices and acts as an internal connection between all office levels.

Collection management is in charge of tracking all art arriving at and departing from the Museum, the movement of art within the Museum, the safe storage of the art, and its conservation. We have split collection management between the basement (at the bottom of the art-storage tower) and the sixth floor. Located at the bottom are Shipping and Receiving, the Registrars' Office, and a portion of the Art Handlers' Offices. On the sixth floor are the Registrars' Offices, the Art Handlers' area (including the viewing room), Rights and Reproductions, Photography, Conservation, and the study storage area.

The curatorial offices are located on several levels in the southwest quadrant of the Museum. With its own internal stair, roof garden, and access to the relocated Wilbour Library, this area will have the feeling of being a curatorial village. From the sixth-floor reception area, curators have direct access to collection management and the storage tower. The Library on the fifth floor, a semi-public area, is easily accessible to both the public and curators for daily use.

4.1. South elevation of model, 1" = 40'.
4.2. Project analytique.
4.3. Overall site plan, 1" = 100'.
4.4. Site and Piano Nobile plans, 1"=40'.
4.5. Piano Nobile, 1"=20'.
4.6 First- and second-floor plans, 1"=40'. First floor: Public entry, Education, food services, art storage, Conservation, Registration, and parking. Second floor: Education, retail shops, galleries, art storage, Conservation, Registration, and mechanical.

The Director's offices and board room are given the symbolically important location on the top floor over the hemicycle in the south facade. These rooms have the grand axial view to the south over the grounds of the Botanic Garden.

Public Education, Shops, and Restaurants. The Brooklyn Museum's dedication to education has historically set it apart from other institutions of its kind. The master-plan design had to accommodate both children's and adults' groups, and nighttime programs. Consequently, we have maintained the present entry lobby on the ground floor as the main entrance for groups that come by bus and subway. Here, visitors can have direct access to the education wing, auditorium, media center, and cafeteria. A night entrance from the garage opens onto the ground floor as well.

The visitor and employee cafeteria is located in one of the most striking rooms in the Museum: under the glass-tile floor of the Beaux-Arts Court. This hypostyle space will be filled with sunlight filtering down from above. The classrooms, seminar rooms, and education offices are located on two levels around the cafeteria, while the auditorium and media center are reached by a north-south hall on the ground level located directly beneath the Great Hall. This grouping of classrooms, cafeteria, and larger congregation spaces forms a discrete nighttime campus that easily ties into the gallery floors during regular Museum hours.

The Museum shops have been located on a balcony that overlooks the cafeteria on three sides and is connected with the main gallery floor on the second level. Because this balcony is directly accessible from the north entrance, it is not necessary to cross through the Museum in order to visit the shops. The visual connection between the cafeteria and the shops will reinforce the patronage of both.

The full-service restaurant, located on the southeast side of the fifth floor, takes full advantage of the southern views. Exterior colonnaded rooftop terraces are available for summer outdoor dining.

Conclusion. We have designed for The Brooklyn Museum a modern building that works both functionally and aesthetically. The institution has been provided with what it needs most: safe yet accessible storage for art; open, large-scale, flexible gallery space; excellent working conditions for the staff; and spatial legibility for the public. The phasing of the construction of the master plan has been carefully orchestrated so that with each step the Museum will be substantially improved. The design is heroic yet realizable, giving The Brooklyn Museum a unified vision to carry it into the next century.

4.7. Piano Nobile, mezzanine, and fourth-floor plans, 1″=40′. Piano Nobile: public entry, galleries, art storage, Conservation, and Registration. Mezzanine: galleries and offices. Fourth floor: galleries, offices, art storage, Conservation, and Registration.
4.8. Fifth-floor plan, east-west section, and sixth-floor plan, 1″=40′. Fifth floor: galleries, food services, Library and research, offices, art storage, Conservation, and Registration. Sixth floor: offices, art storage, Conservation, and Registration.
4.9. Basement, second parking level, and roof plans, 1″=40′. Basement: art storage, Conservation, Registration, mechanical, Operations, and parking.
4.10. Garden elevation, ³⁄₃₂″=1′, and site section, 1″=20′.
4.11. West elevation, east elevation, and cross section, 1″=20′.
4.12. Section details, ³⁄₁₆″=1′.

THE
BROOKLYN MUSEUM
MASTER PLAN

ATKIN VOITH & ASSOCIATES ARCHITECTS
ROTHZEID KAISERMAN THOMSON & BEE   GOLDMAN SOKOLOW AND COPELAND
JOHN MILNER ASSOCIATES   JOSEPH M CHAPMAN   KEAST AND HOOD COMPANY
ARENA AND COMPANY   WALMSLEY AND COMPANY   GEORGE IZENOUR

4.2

ATKIN
VOITH
&
ASSOC
RKTAS

THE BROOKLYN MUSEUM MASTER PLAN
SITE PLAN   1"=100'-0"

4.3

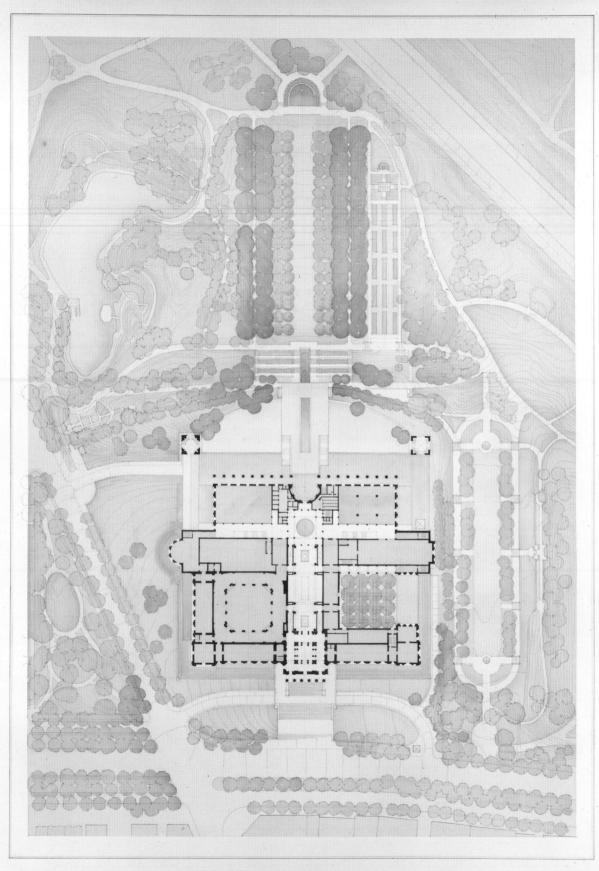

THE BROOKLYN MUSEUM MASTER PLAN
SITE PLAN   1" = 40'-0"

4.4

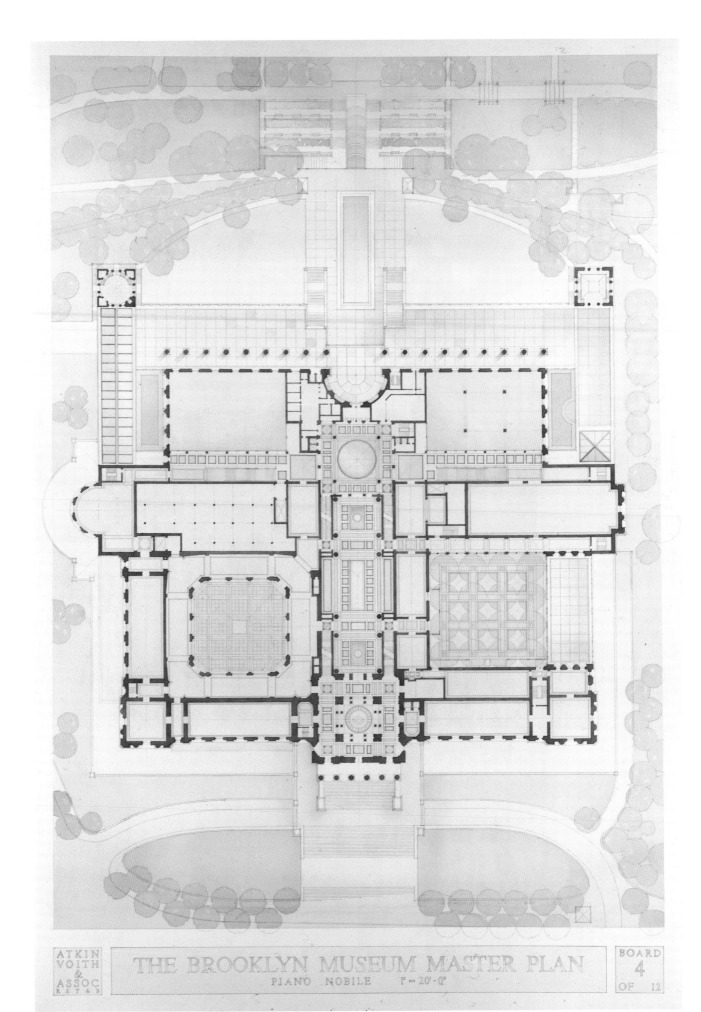

ATKIN
VOITH
&
ASSOC
RET4S

4.5

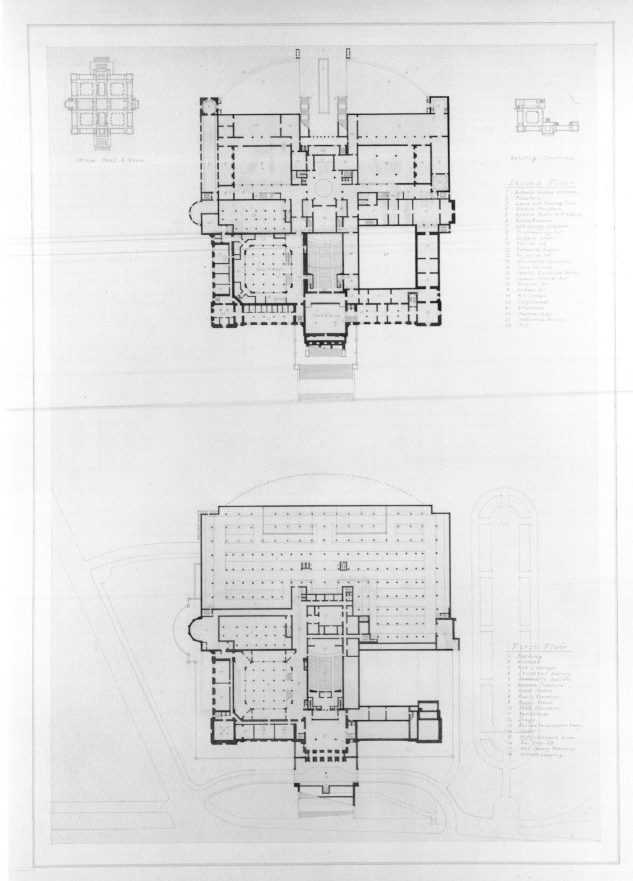

THE BROOKLYN MUSEUM MASTER PLAN

FIRST AND SECOND FLOOR PLANS   1" = 40'-0"

BOARD
5
OF 12

4.6

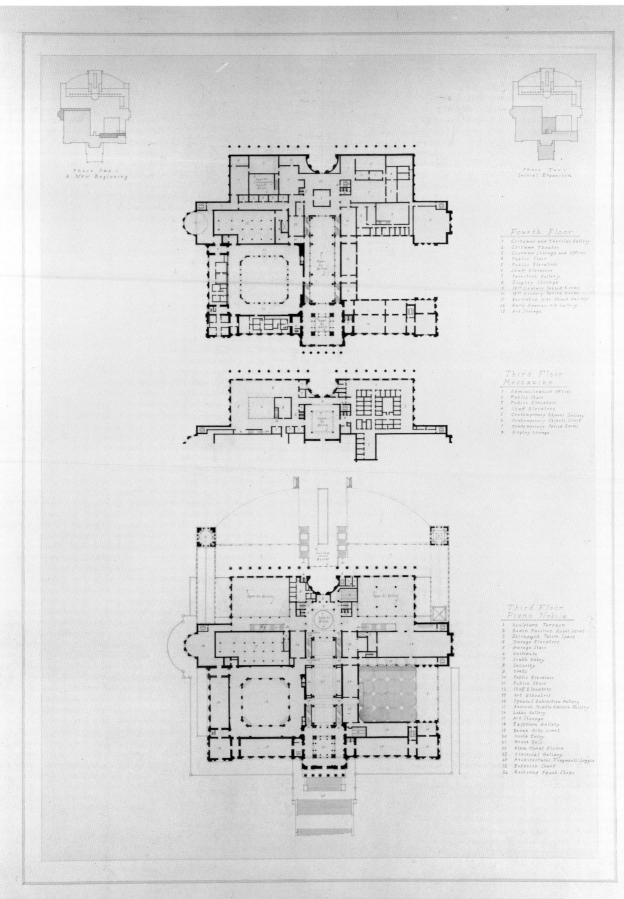

4.7

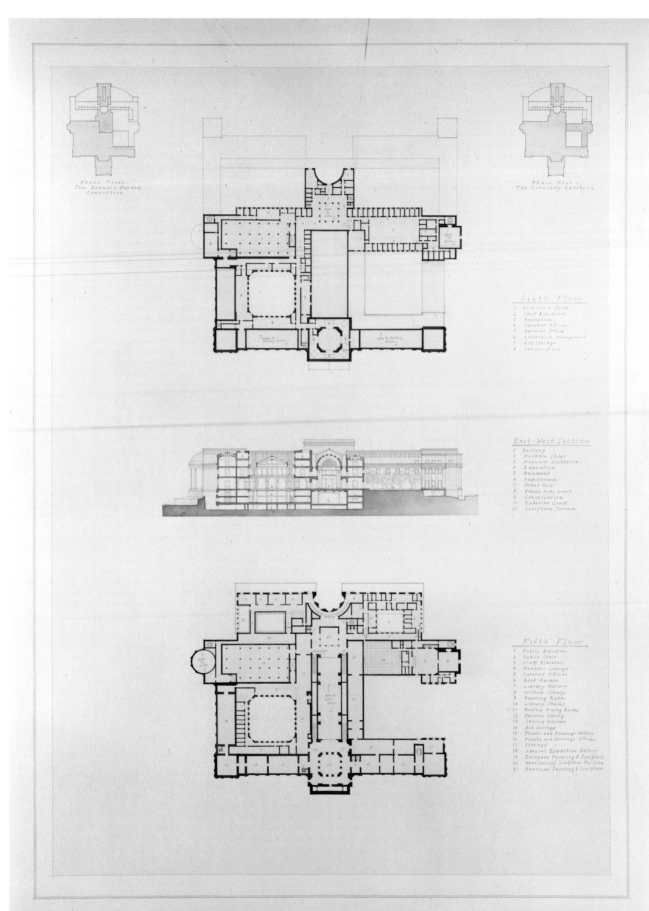

ATKIN
VOITH
&
ASSOC.
ΕΚΤΒΒ

THE BROOKLYN MUSEUM MASTER PLAN

FIFTH FLOOR PLAN, EAST-WEST SECTION AND SIXTH FLOOR PLAN 1" = 40'-0"

4.8

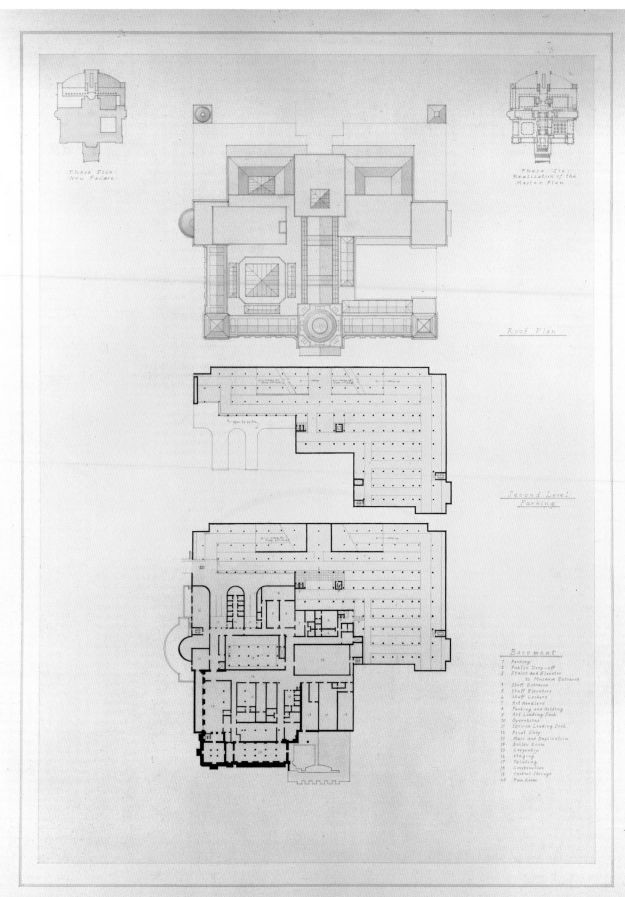

Phase Five:
New Façade

Phase Six:
Realization of the
Master Plan

Roof Plan

Second Level
Parking

Basement

1   Parking
2   Public Drop-off
3   Stairs and Elevator
    to Museum Entrance
4   Staff Entrance
5   Staff Elevators
6   Staff Lockers
7   Art Handling
8   Parking and Holding
9   Art Loading Dock
10 Operations
11 Service Loading Dock
12 Print Shop
13 Mail and Duplication
14 Boiler Room
15 Carpentry
16 Staging
17 Painting
18 Construction
19 Central Storage
20 Fan Room

THE BROOKLYN MUSEUM MASTER PLAN
BASEMENT, SECOND PARKING LEVEL AND ROOF PLANS   1" = 40'-0"

ATKIN
VOITH
&
ASSOC.
RKTAS

BOARD
8
OF 12

4.9

SEUM MASTER PLAN

AND   SITE   SECTION   1"= 20'-0"

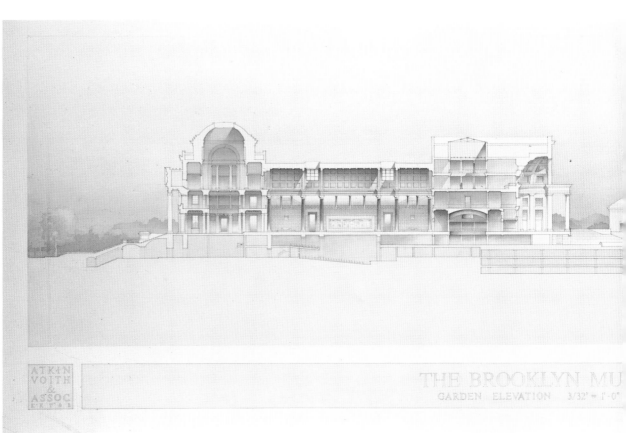

THE BROOKLYN MU
GARDEN ELEVATION 3/32" = 1'-0"

4.10

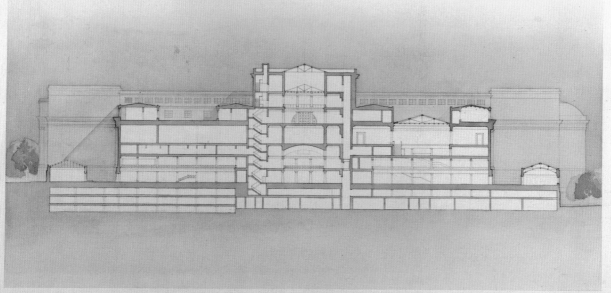

ATKIN
VOITH
&
ASSOC
R K T & B

BOARD
11
OF 12

THE BROOKLYN MUSEUM MASTER PLAN
SIDE ELEVATIONS AND CROSS SECTION   1" = 20'-0"

Totem Pavilion

Contemporary
Objects Court

South Entry

Architectural
Fragments Court

Rodin Pavilion

ATKIN
VOITH
&
ASSOC
RKT&S

THE BROOKLYN MUSEUM MASTER PLAN
SECTION DETAILS   3/16" = 1'-0"

BOARD
12
OF 12

4.12

Kohn Pedersen Fox

Team
William Pedersen
David M. Leventhal
David Diamond
Joel Sanders
Hitoshi Amano
Alan Aranoff
Christopher Bardt
Joshua Chaiken
J. William Davis
Peter Dixon
Michel Freudiger
Genevieve Gormley

Grace Kobayashi
Elaine Newman
Andrew Pollack
Ilona Rider
Thomas Shafer
Model Makers
Peter Menderson
Robert Guillot
Photographer
Jock Pottle
Cost Estimator
V. J. Desai

4.13

William Pedersen

William Pedersen, AIA, Partner in Charge of Design, is an architect with more than twenty years of design experience. Prior to the formation of Kohn Pedersen Fox Associates, he was Vice President at John Carl Warnecke & Associates, and senior designer at I. M. Pei & Partners and Pietro Belluschi. His work has been featured in the *AIA Journal, Architectural Record, Baumeister, L'Architettura, A + U Magazine, Newsweek, Leaders Magazine, Global Architecture, Progressive Architecture,* and *Vanity Fair*, as well as in *The New York Times, The Wall Street Journal,* and *The Chicago Tribune.* Mr. Pedersen has also been published in *The New Art Examiner* ("Architecture and Praxis: A Self-Analysis of the Essential Criteria for the Urban Skyscraper") and *Southwest Center: The Houston Competition* ("Considerations for Urban Architecture and the Tall Building").

Recipient of the Rome Prize in Architecture in 1965, Mr. Pedersen is a fellow of the American Academy in Rome. In 1985, he and his partner Arthur May were awarded the Brunner Memorial Prize by the American Academy and the National Institute of Arts and Letters. He has received numerous AIA design awards, including the 1984 National Honor Award for 333 Wacker Drive, Chicago.

Mr. Pedersen has served on design-award juries of the New York, Nebraska, Minnesota, Iowa, Washington, D.C., Philadelphia, and Chicago chapters of the American Institute of Architects and also juried the AIA Residential Design Award of New York. He has also served on design juries at Cornell University, the Urban Design Studio at Cornell University, Columbia University, Harvard University Graduate School of Design, Yale University, Princeton University, University of California at Los Angeles, and the Rhode Island School of Design. He has taught at many universities, including RISD, Harvard, and Columbia. Mr. Pedersen has lectured nationwide and has been a guest speaker at the University of Utah, Cornell, Yale, the University of Illinois Chicago Circle Campus, Harvard, the Architectural League of New York, the Walker Art Center in Minneapolis, and the San Francisco Museum of Art. He also served as a panelist at the 1983 NEOCON International Design Seminar.

Mr. Pedersen attended the University of Minnesota, where he received a bachelor of architecture degree in 1961. He received his master of architecture degree at the Massachusetts Institute of Technology in 1963, where he was awarded a Whitney Fellowship.

David M. Leventhal, AIA, Senior Designer, has been with Kohn Pedersen Fox Associates since 1980 and is an Associate Partner at the firm. He was senior designer for the Bucknell University Performing Arts Center Project and was responsible for the design of office buildings in New York, Boston, and Chicago. Prior to joining Kohn Pedersen Fox, he worked briefly for Cain, Farrell, & Bell, the successor firm to McKim, Mead & White.

Mr. Leventhal received his master's degree in architecture from Harvard University, where he also studied fine arts as an undergraduate. Prior to taking his degree in architecture, he worked as a curatorial assistant at the Fogg Art Museum in Cambridge, Massachusetts, and at The Metropolitan Museum of Art in New York.

David Diamond, Senior Designer, has been with Kohn Pedersen Fox Associates since 1983. He was senior designer for a mixed-use tower at 712 Fifth Avenue, New York, and a designer for ABC Phase II, a new studio and office building on West 66th Street, New York. Before joining Kohn Pedersen Fox Associates, he was a designer for Richard Meier and Partners, where he worked on the Museum für Kunsthandwerk in Frankfurt and the High Museum of Art in Atlanta.

A recipient of the ITT International Fellowship to Italy in 1979, Mr. Diamond studied architecture and urban design in Rome. He received his master's degree in architecture from Cornell University and his bachelor's degree in architecture from The Cooper Union.

Project Description

The dictionary defines a museum as a place for learned occupation, an institution devoted to the procurement, care, study, and display of objects of lasting interest or value, a place where objects are exhibited. A museum is a repository for artifacts. As such, a museum with its collection is a microcosm of society. It thus reflects the ideals and aspirations of society. Karl-Friedrich Schinkel's Altes Museum in Berlin, in its highly centralized and austerely ordered plan, reflects the early nineteenth-century fascination with order and antiquity. Classical sculptures are arranged in the central drum, the focus of the museum and the organizing element of the plan.

In a similar manner, McKim, Mead & White's master plan for The Brooklyn Institute of Arts and Sciences is a perfect expression of society's aspirations and ideals at the turn of the century in Brooklyn. The McKim plan expresses the monumental role of the institution. It reflects the nineteenth-century obsession with placing all things and organizing the universe into a single comprehensive pattern. Although only a small fragment of the plan was built, it would be a mistake today to simply continue the plan in its original form. In certain ways the institution has pared down and simplified itself; no longer does it include a natural-history museum or a school. In other ways both its role in society and the demands of its setting have grown more complex. The neighborhood has grown; Mount Prospect Park and the Brooklyn Botanic Garden have been built.

The Botanic Garden, created after the McKim, Mead & White plan, most profoundly affects the development of the new master plan. The Garden is a delightful collection of discrete episodes without an explicit ordering sequence. One such episode, the Cherry Esplanade, is a formal and axially ordered garden room—a complete and idealized world within itself, peaceful and satisfying. Another, the column on the Osborne Terrace, represents a Romantic notion of ruin within the landscape—a reminder of past greatness now eroded by the forces of nature. A third, the rose garden, is a highly ordered and decorative pattern. It provides an image for contemplation or delight. Thus, on the one hand, there is the remnant of a Museum plan that was a symbol of the nineteenth-century sense of order. On the other hand there is the Garden, expressing both the variety of the natural world and an overall pattern within which a range of ideals function as separate episodes.

The essence of the problem is to resolve the connection between Museum and Garden. What should this intersection mean and what physical form should it take? One could impose a single overwhelming order implying that a single answer can be provided: a Versailles. Or one could draw out the ordering systems inherent in the fragments, completing those implied, transforming some, and inventing others. One could link these systems in a way that permits overlap, ambiguity, complexity, and richness. The prototype could be Hadrian's Villa. This is the direction we have chosen.

We have organized our plan around a journey from city to garden to art, a sequence that weaves those systems into the new master plan. The process became one of extending the fragments and weaving together a whole through completion, transformation, or contrast. The plan of the original scheme is remembered but not fully occupied. The four-quadrant organization is retained but transformed. In section, one sees the court in quadrant 2 as a void within the solid of the museum. In quadrant 3 it is transformed into a solid object, a pavilion for restaurants in the garden. This in fact is also a transformation of one of the greenhouse structures that stand in the Botanic Garden. In quadrant 4, the edge between Museum and Garden has been blurred, and the zone between the two becomes imbued with qualities of both. The original plan is both eroded and completed by the Garden. The fourth tower—a fragment of the McKim, Mead & White plan—

becomes the memory of that older plan embraced by the Garden. It is literally a ruin, and in fact is the place where the Museum's architectural fragments are lodged. The theme of erosion describes the transition and the balance between man-made and natural.

We have thus woven together a new order. All these experiences are strung together through the central stair hall that is the great interior public space. This articulates the preferred path from city to garden to art as well as permitting varied alternative sequences. It is along this path that the Museum reveals its collections to the visitor. The organizing device is the continuing journey itself as opposed to the single-focus centralized space of the original plan. No single collection occupies the central focal point in the Museum plan. The very essence of the Museum is the diversity of the collections. The artifact of one culture cannot be used as a center point for others. The great ascending staircase of the wall, reminiscent of a garden ruin, is itself a repository for architectural fragments.

A comparison of the facades shows the variety inherent in our scheme. Where the north is formal and symmetrical and speaks with a Classical vocabulary, the south reveals the many disparate elements of the plan. The west elevation represents the initial transformation from old to new. The framework of the old is repeated and infilled with the slate of the garden. The east elevation expresses the final transformation in which elements are contrasted, juxtaposed, and overlapped.

In conclusion, the master plan provides a comprehensive unifying framework that allows each individual episode to maintain its integrity and participate in the overall pattern. It continues and complements what existed, expressing symmetry and asymmetry, order and freedom, the Classic and the Romantic.

109

4.13. South elevation of model, 1″ = 40′.
4.14. Overall site plan, 1″ = 100′.
4.15. Site and Piano Nobile plans, 1″ = 40′.
4.16. Piano Nobile, 1″ = 20′.
4.17. Roof and basement plans, 1″ = 40′. Basement: public entry, Education, art storage, Conservation, Registration, mechanical, Operations, and parking.
4.18. First- and second-floor plans, 1″ = 40′. First floor: Education, Library and research, art storage, Conservation, and Registration.

Second floor: public entry, Education, retail shops, galleries, food services, and offices.
4.19. Third- and fourth-floor plans, 1″ = 40′. Third floor: public entry, Education, galleries, and food services. Fourth floor: galleries.
4.20. Fifth- and sixth-floor plans, 1″ = 40′. Fifth floor: galleries. Sixth floor: offices, art storage, Conservation, and Registration.
4.21. Sections and elevations, 1″ = 40′, and longitudinal section, 3/32″ = 1′.
4.22. Longitudinal site section and axonometric rendering, 1″ = 40′.

THE BROOKLYN MVSEVM
MASTER PLAN COMPETITION

SITE PLAN

1" = 100'

MCMLXXXVI

KOHN   PEDERSEN   FOX

4.14

THE BROOKLYN MVSEVM
MASTER PLAN COMPETITION

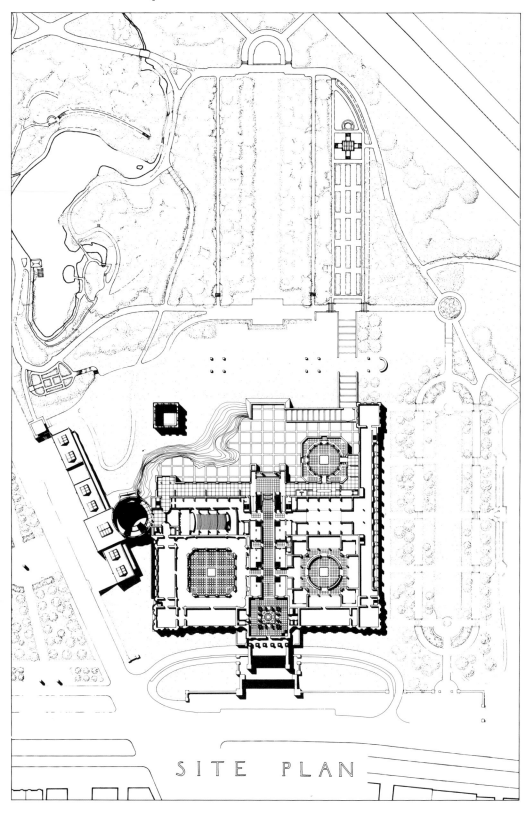

SITE PLAN

MCMLXXXVI

KOHN PEDERSEN FOX

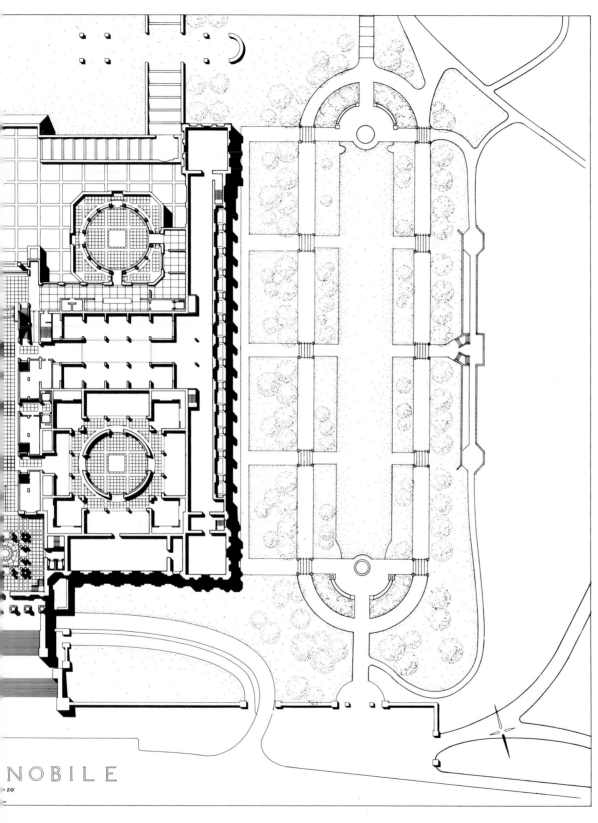

NOBILE
20'

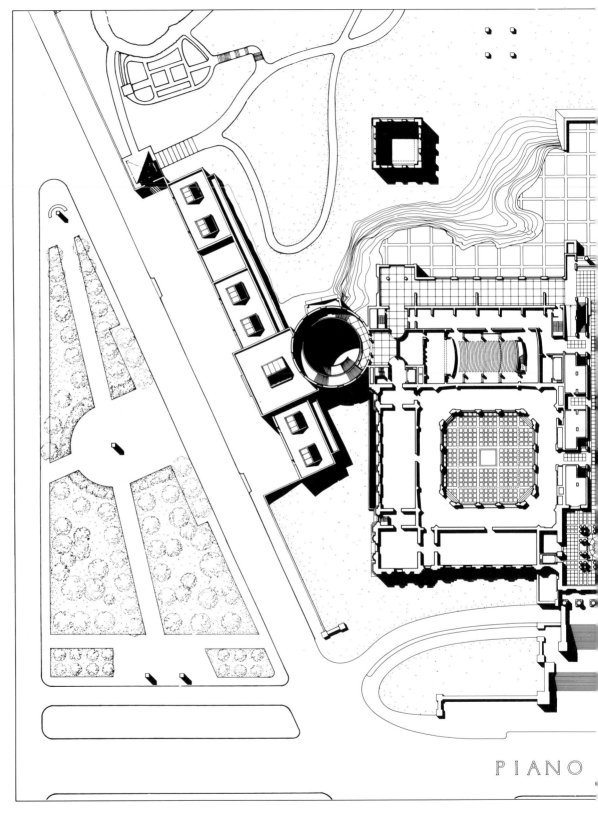

PIANO

MCML

KOHN PED

THE BROOKLYN MVSEVM
MASTER PLAN COMPETITION

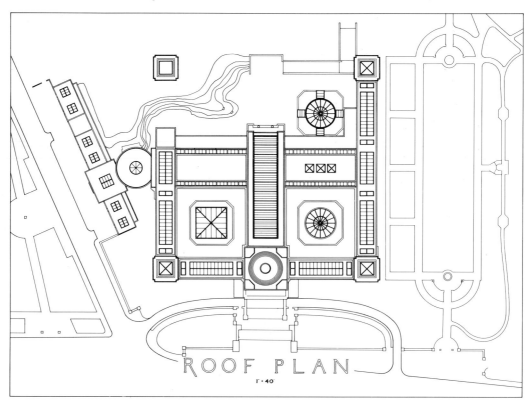

ROOF PLAN

1"=40'

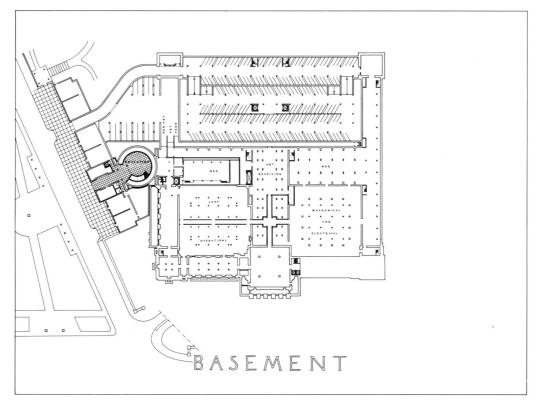

BASEMENT

MCMLXXXVI

KOHN   PEDERSEN   FOX

THE BROOKLYN MVSEVM
MASTER PLAN COMPETITION

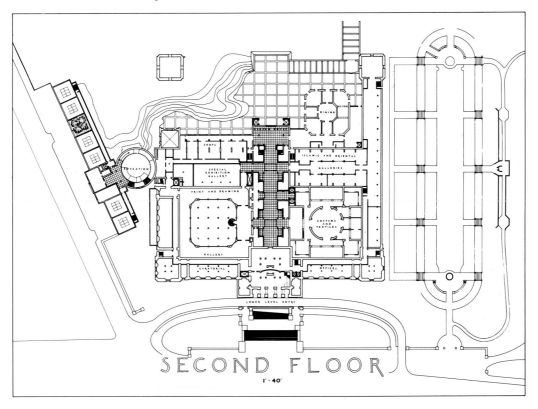

SECOND FLOOR
1' - 40'

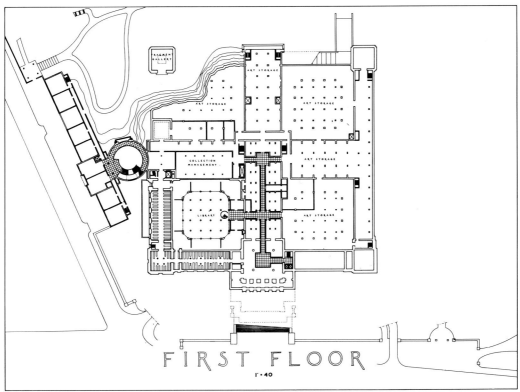

FIRST FLOOR
1' - 40

MCMLXXXVI

KOHN PEDERSEN FOX

4.18

YN MVSEVM
COMPETITION

SOVTH ELEVATION

1" · 40'

ON A

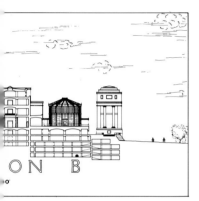

ON B

WEST ELEVATION

1" · 40'

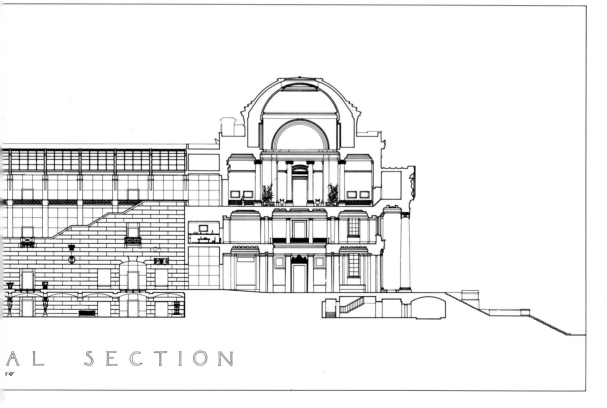

AL SECTION

1'·0"

XXXVI

RSEN FOX

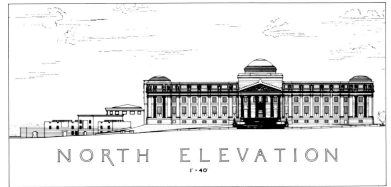

NORTH ELEVATION

1" = 40'

SECTI

EAST ELEVATION

1" = 40'

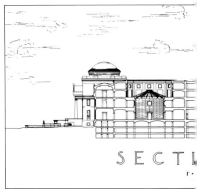

SECTI

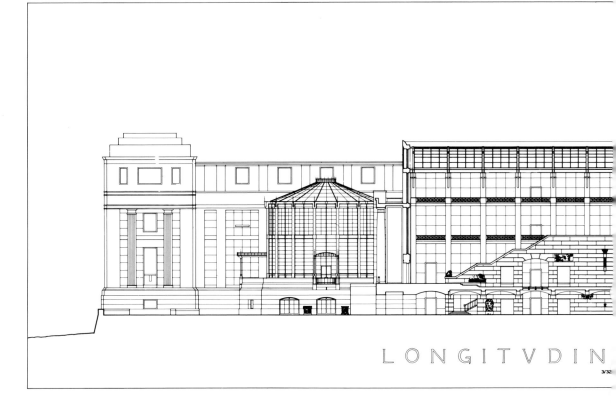

LONGITVDIN

3/32

MCML

KOHN PED

4.21

THE BROOKLYN MVSEVM
MASTER PLAN COMPETITION

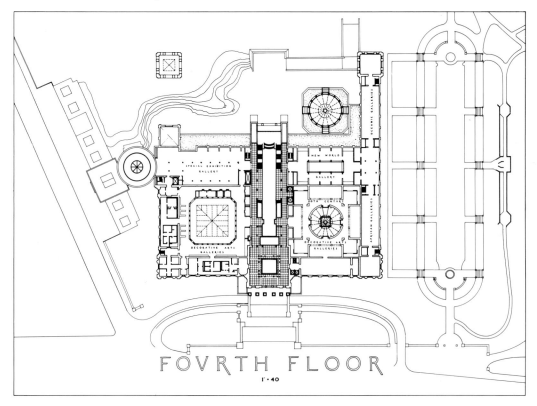

FOVRTH FLOOR
1" • 40'

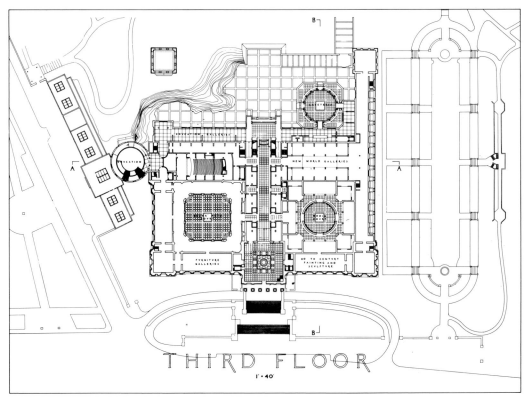

THIRD FLOOR
1" • 40'

MCMLXXXVI

KOHN PEDERSEN FOX

THE BROOKLYN MVSEVM
MASTER PLAN COMPETITION

SIXTH FLOOR
1' • 40

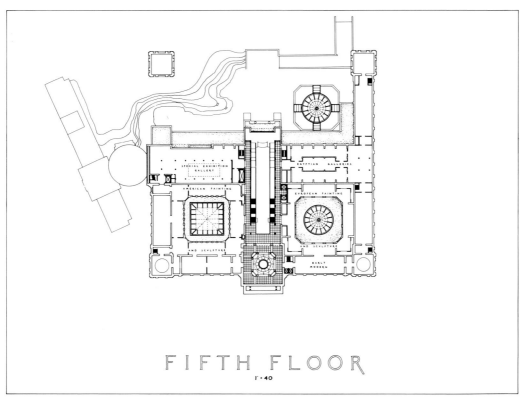

FIFTH FLOOR
1' • 40

MCMLXXXVI

KOHN PEDERSEN FOX

SITE SECTION

40'

PERSPECTIVE

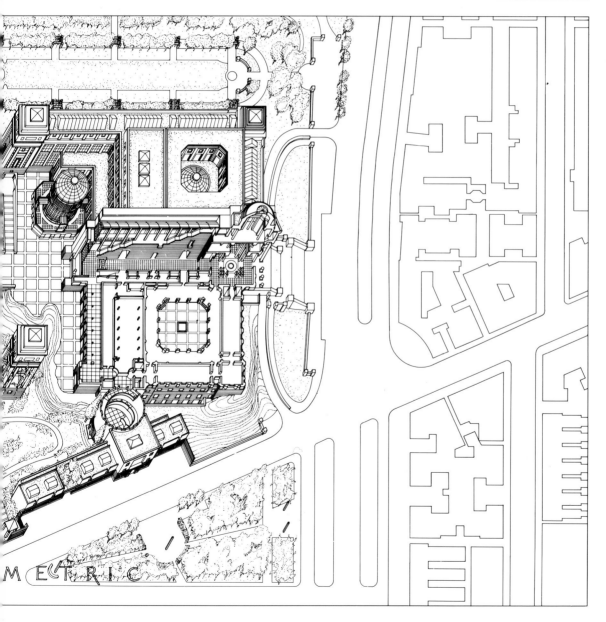

METRIC

XXXVI

ERSEN FOX

PERSPECTIVE

LONGITVDINAL

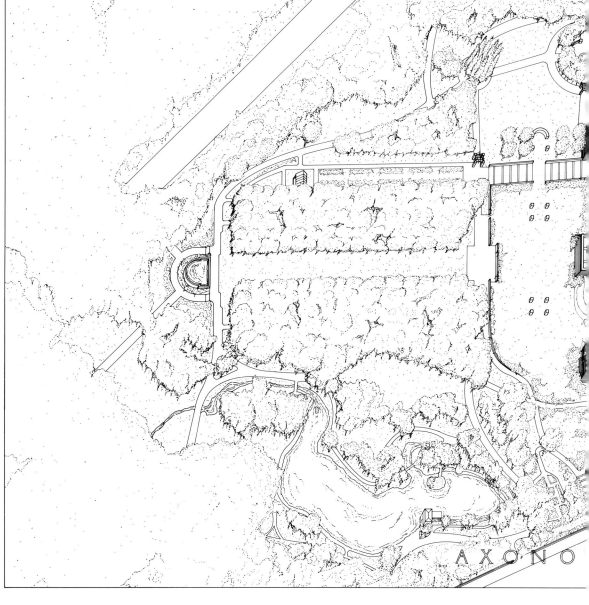

A X O N O

MCML

KOHN   PED

4.22

**Skidmore, Owings & Merrill with
The Vitetta Group/Studio Four**

Team
David M. Childs
Marilyn Jordan Taylor
Thomas Fridstein
James L. Bodnar
Roger Duffy
Tad Berezowski
Stephanie Gelb
Jason Gold
Gary Haney
Imrana Inayatullah
Drew Kepley
Timothy Love
Gillian Luck

Richard Metsky
Sergio Paz
Stan Pszczolkowski
Mark Regulinski
Dan Shannon
Jose Solis
Marcella Villanueva
Studio Four Team
Hyman Myers
William T. Bowers
James R. Keller
Joseph W. Sorrentino, Jr.
Model Team
Harold Gilstein

Nancy Aldrich
Dan Colina
Carolyn Blythe Fleet
Jeffrey Gross
Richard Hopper
William Liechter
Tzyy-Hann Liu
Timothy Owens
Graphics
Steve Thomas
Mike Abes
Other
Jane Morris
Bonnie Yee

Marion Cooper
Landscape Architecture
Michael Sardina, SWA
Lighting
Paul Marantz, Jules Fisher
   & Paul Marantz, Inc.

David M. Childs

Skidmore, Owings & Merrill, a partnership with offices in New York, Washington, Boston, Chicago, Houston, Denver, San Francisco, Los Angeles, and London, has long been in the forefront of the architectural community. This leadership has been recognized in the granting of numerous design awards, including the American Institute of Architect's first Architectural Firm Award, in 1962, for excellence in design. Since Skidmore, Owings & Merrill's founding the firm has undertaken a variety of projects in the United States and in more than forty countries thoughout the world.

David M. Childs, FAIA, Design Partner in the New York office of Skidmore, Owings & Merrill, received a bachelor of arts degree from Yale College in 1963 and a master of architecture degree from Yale University's Graduate School of Architecture in 1967. He joined Skidmore, Owings & Merrill in 1971 and became a partner in 1975. Respected for his involvement in design projects throughout the East Coast, Mr. Childs has served as Executive Director of the Pennsylvania Avenue Commission and Chairman of the National Capital Planning Commission in Washington, D.C. He has led the firm's design in many projects in historical settings, including the Washington Mall; the Constitution Gardens adjoining the Mall; historic train stations in Washington, D.C., Baltimore, Wilmington, Philadelphia, Newark, New Haven, New London, Providence, and Boston; Worldwide Plaza, a mixed-use complex on the site of the old Madison Square Garden, New York; and South Ferry, a design competition for the rebuilding of the Ferry Terminal and the development of a mixed-use complex at the southern tip of Manhattan.

Marilyn Jordan Taylor, Urban Design Partner at Skidmore, Owings & Merrill, received her bachelor of arts degree from Harvard University in 1969 and her master of architecture degree from the University of California at Berkeley in 1974. She joined the firm in 1971 and became a partner in 1986.

Her design responsibilities have included the Northeast Corridor Improvement Project, a federal initiative that led to the investment of over $250 million in thirteen train stations, including those of Washington, D.C., New York, and Boston; the award-winning Capital Center Plan and Development Criteria for Providence; master planning for sixty air-rights acres at 30th Street Station, Philadelphia; Worldwide Plaza; the Skidmore, Owings & Merrill submission for the South Ferry competition; and the addition of a people-mover system and a new Midfield Concourse at Dulles International Airport, Washington, D.C.

For The Brooklyn Museum Master Plan Competition, Skidmore, Owings & Merrill joined with The Vitetta Group/Studio Four, a Philadelphia-based architecture firm with extensive experience in museum restoration. Hyman Myers, a senior partner and the chief restoration architect of The Vitetta Group/Studio Four, received a bachelor of architectural engineering degree in 1963 and a master of architecture degree in 1965 from the University of Pennsylvania. He is nationally recognized for his expertise in adaptive reuse and restoration of historic architecture. He has been deeply involved in the preservation and restoration of historic landmarks and has won numerous awards for his work.

As director of Studio Four, Mr. Myers has overall responsibility for the design development and documentation of projects involving the rehabilitation and reuse of existing buildings. He has also developed numerous feasibility studies concerned with the reuse of old buildings. Projects that Mr. Myers has directed include a complete renovation of the 1876 building of The Pennsylvania Academy of the Fine Arts, Philadelphia; the complete renovation and restoration of various galleries and office space in the West Building of The National Gallery of Art, Washington, D.C.; ongoing restoration and renovation services for the Academy of Music, Philadelphia, a national historic landmark; and master planning for the Winterthur Museum complex in Delaware. Mr. Myers has lectured nationally on the subject of preservation, has been active nationally on preservation committees and boards, and has served on several historic commissions. He has also taught in the preservation program at the University of Pennsylvania.

125

Project Description

We propose for The Brooklyn Museum a master plan that formally and dramatically integrates setting, Garden, Museum, and activity. Our master plan provides a series of carefully conceived circulation paths and an architecturally ordered sequence of spaces, interior and exterior, through which to enjoy the Museum and its grounds. The circulation paths and the spaces they link are of equal importance to the design; together they give the Museum both the interest of fine-grained texture and the order of large-scale organizational clarity.

The original McKim, Mead & White master plan was a bold step in planning for the needs and goals of the Museum, laying the groundwork for its physical growth and direction. Although the original master plan was never fully realized and only a small portion of the plan actually constructed, the monumental building that did result remains an important influence on the Museum. Our master plan for The Brooklyn Museum is intended to create an appropriate presence for an architecturally ordered "collection of spaces" in which to house the "collection of collections" that is The Brooklyn Museum.

Objectives for The Brooklyn Museum Master Plan

1. To give the Museum a clear organization, integrating presently disjointed masses, meeting needs for adjacency and separation, and providing orientation for the patron no matter where he is in the complex.

2. To unite Eastern Parkway, the Botanic Garden, and the Museum as a single urban composition intended to reinforce their collective and individual importance to the city. The Museum becomes an entrance to the Garden and the Garden an entrance to the Museum, each institution enhanced by the other.

3. To extend the Classical Beaux-Arts principles that are clearly established by the original plan, yet express them in a newer architectural language, in which void, glass, and incidental and functional asymmetries can be introduced to enrich the overall formal plan.

4. To address the needs of the community, with active relationships between exterior and interior spaces and with after-hours and education facilities easily and directly accessible.

5. To provide for phased change, using early stages to increase gallery and storage space and to balance the mass of the building.

The Design Proposal. Our proposed design responds respectfully to the existing McKim, Mead & White master plan, expanding on the original concept of axial corridors and skylit courts as organizing elements in the building. The design is organized around a "central spine," which begins with the existing domed Entrance Pavilion that addresses Eastern Parkway. The Entrance Pavilion leads to a new exterior garden, a cloister lined by glass walls that enclose stairs, escalators, and bridges that link the gallery floors of the Museum. This cloister becomes a void that organizes the Museum into its East and West Wings. It also brings the Garden into the Museum and provides a direct visual connection to the Brooklyn Botanic Garden to the south.

This new spine is at once the formal entrance to the Museum and the formal entrance to the Garden. It is here that a combination of original building and new building come together to form symbolically the "new" Museum, linking the past and the future.

Two circulation systems intertwine through the central spine. The Museum circulation begins at Eastern Parkway and rises via restored but reconfigured monumental stairs to the Piano Nobile's Grand Foyer. To form the Foyer, the third and fourth floors of the Entrance Pavilion are reconfigured as in the original building plans; a glazed opening also provides visual connection to the first floor below. From the Foyer, one proceeds to the South Porch, which encloses the Lobby Galleries and provides access to the Museum. There one sees the Garden Cloister, extending to the south. Within its walls, stairs rise beside the East Wing and escalators beside the West Wing, leading to the galleries and to a fifth-floor bridge. From the southern end of the cloister, loggias extend to define the Garden Ellipse, a Museum garden that leads to the Botanic Garden beyond.

The Garden circulation also begins at Eastern Parkway, from which it provides a free pathway through exterior Museum spaces to the Botanic Garden. Along the path, Museum objects are displayed and views to interior Museum spaces offered, encouraging passersby to come in on their next visit. To reach this path, one enters either in the opening at the center of the monumental stairs or at the porte cochere. At the Entrance Pavilion, the passage flows through the central space formed by columns and up a ramp to the exterior space of the Garden Cloister. From the Garden Cloister, one passes beneath the bridges linking the East and West Wings to the Garden Ellipse, from which entry to the Botanic Garden can be made. This free access between the Museum and Botanic Garden responds to their "shared" site relationship. The Museum now sits comfortably in a larger gar- 127 den, and the Botanic Garden has a clear focus and a new meaningful location for its new main entrance.

Entrance to the Museum for special users is generally at the lower level of the Entrance Pavilion. Schoolchildren, community groups, and auditorium audiences will enter through the porte cochere and gain direct access to the Education Department in the East Wing or to the new auditorium directly ahead. Access for the handicapped is also provided at this level, where elevators connect to the Grand Foyer. Patrons entering from the new 1,000-space parking garage will use two stair courts to reach the Garden Ellipse, where they will proceed along the Garden Cloister to the Entrance Pavilion.

The reconstruction of the great outdoor main stair to the Piano Nobile celebrates and reestablishes the formal entrance into the Museum under the original portico. The restored Foyer just inside the portico, with its reopened square oculus above and the new oculus cut into the floor, visually connects—vertically—the first, second, and fourth floors to the Piano Nobile. The large floor-to-ceiling openings in the south wall of the Foyer also establish a strong visual connection between the Foyer and the Garden Cloister and the Botanic Garden in the distance.

These horizontal and vertical visual connections define the multilevel complexity of the building as well as establish the building's relationship to the outdoor garden, providing a sense of orientation for the visitor. As one passes through the Foyer and enters the new south porch overlooking the Garden Cloister, one becomes aware of the cross axis that links the East and West Wings, connecting the restored Beaux-Arts Court and the new skylit court. The public galleries are organized around these skylit courts in a series of concentric layers. The courts bring daylight to the center of each wing, and each court can be viewed from the surrounding gallery levels, providing a clear sense of interior orientation.

Facing the Garden Ellipse along the south side of the building are additional galleries with gallery arms extending toward the Botanic Garden. These house special exhibition galleries on the Piano Nobile and permanent collection galleries above. The special exhibition areas open onto large reception areas that overlook the Garden Ellipse and provide space for openings, special orientation gatherings, assembly of special tour groups, and other special events. The special exhibition gallery wings terminate in stair pavilions that connect to the permanent galleries above as well as to the cafeteria below.

Architecturally we have sought to add to the landmark building in a manner that respects its original intentions and extends its monumentality—a character appropriate to a major civic institution—but is clearly distinguished from it in its use and detailing of materials: the proportions and bay rhythm of the McKim, Mead & White building are maintained; facade motifs are abstracted; and glass and steel elements are attached to the reductive geometries of the masonry enclosure that houses the galleries. A literal link is made between the Garden and the public spaces by the use of glass, which allows the lightness and the activity of the Museum to be expressed on the exterior, while emphasizing the open relationship between the Museum and the Garden.

THE BROOKLYN MUSEUM
THE COMPLETED MASTER PLAN

THE BROOKLYN MUSEUM MASTER PLAN COMPETITION

DRAWING NO. 1   SEPTEMBER 15, 1986

SKIDMORE, OWINGS & MERRILL • NEW YORK
VITETTA GROUP/STUDIO FOUR

4.24

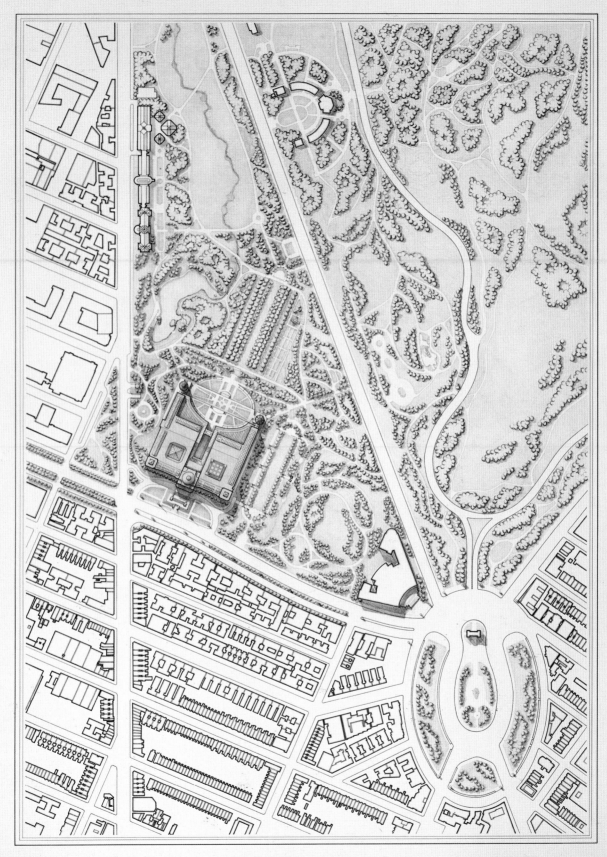

CONTEXT PLAN

THE BROOKLYN MUSEUM MASTER PLAN COMPETITION

DRAWING NO. 2   SEPTEMBER 15, 1986

SKIDMORE, OWINGS & MERRILL • NEW YORK
VITETTA GROUP/STUDIO FOUR

4.25

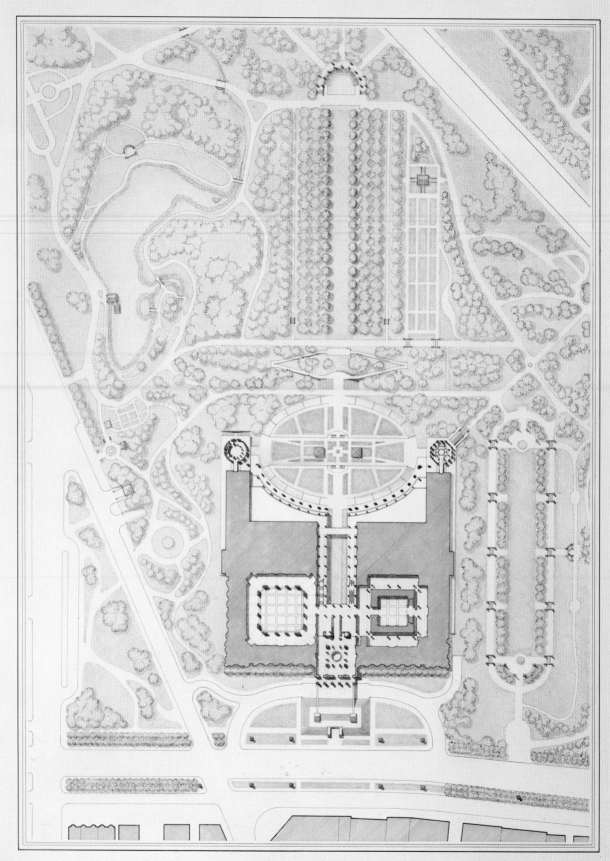

SITE PLAN

THE BROOKLYN MUSEUM MASTER PLAN COMPETITION

DRAWING NO. 3   SEPTEMBER 15, 1986

SKIDMORE, OWINGS & MERRILL • NEW YORK
VITETTA GROUP/STUDIO FOUR

4.26

PIANO NOBILE

THE BROOKLYN MUSEUM MASTER PLAN COMPETITION

DRAWING NO. 4   SEPTEMBER 15, 1986

SKIDMORE, OWINGS & MERRILL • NEW YORK
VITETTA GROUP/STUDIO FOUR

4.27

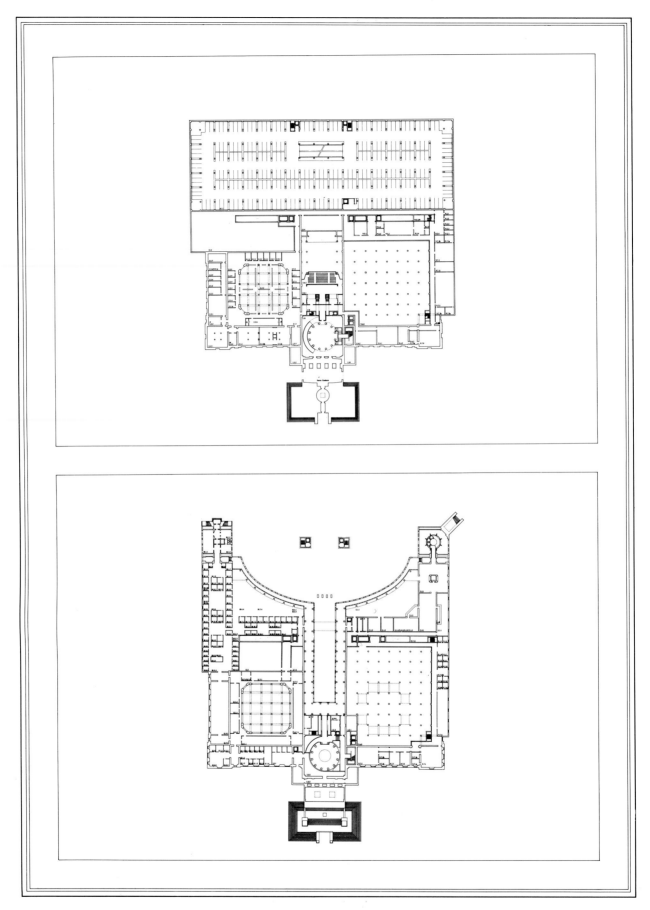

FIRST AND SECOND FLOOR PLANS

THE BROOKLYN MUSEUM MASTER PLAN COMPETITION

DRAWING NO. 5   SEPTEMBER 15, 1986

SKIDMORE, OWINGS & MERRILL • NEW YORK
VITETTA GROUP/STUDIO FOUR

4.28

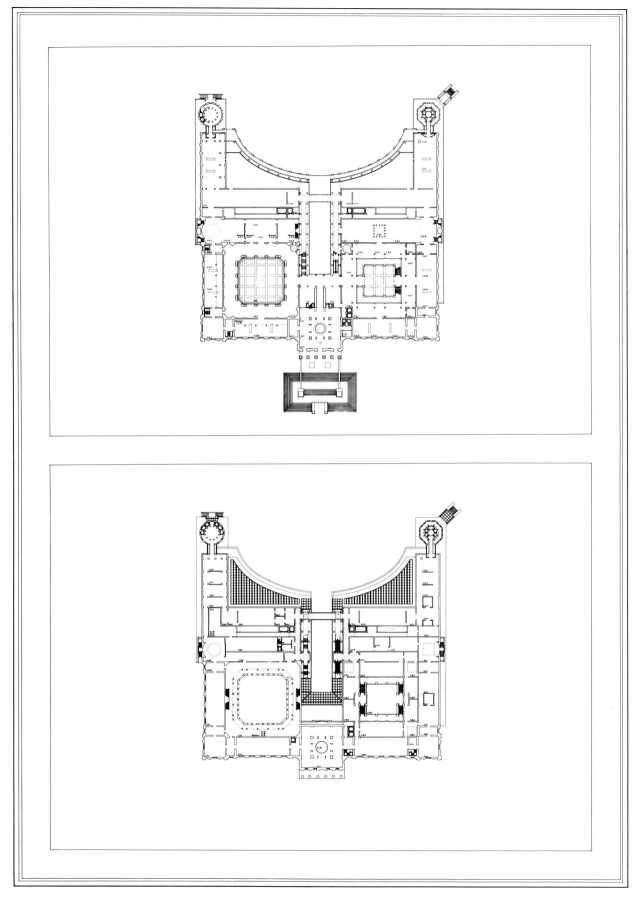

THIRD AND FOURTH FLOOR PLANS

THE BROOKLYN MUSEUM MASTER PLAN COMPETITION

DRAWING NO. 6   SEPTEMBER 15, 1986

SKIDMORE, OWINGS & MERRILL • NEW YORK
VITETTA GROUP/STUDIO FOUR

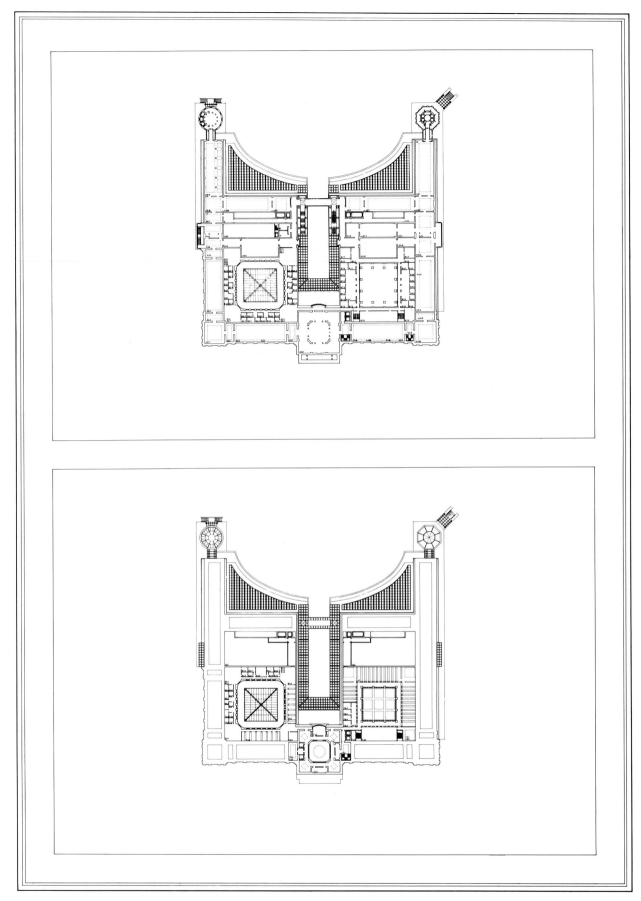

FIFTH AND SIXTH FLOOR PLANS

THE BROOKLYN MUSEUM MASTER PLAN COMPETITION

DRAWING NO. 7   SEPTEMBER 15, 1986

SKIDMORE, OWINGS & MERRILL · NEW YORK
VITETTA GROUP/STUDIO FOUR

4.30

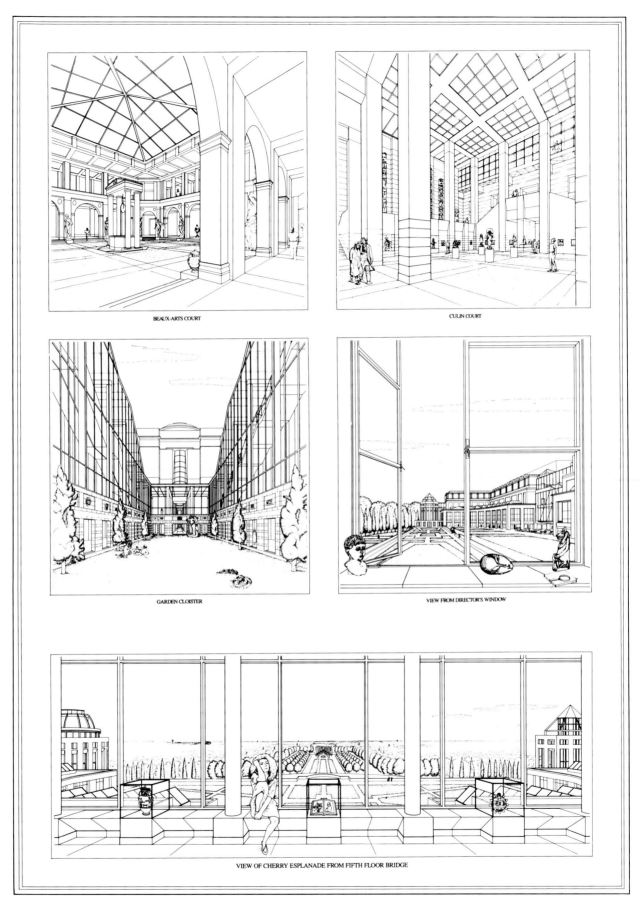

BEAUX-ARTS COURT

CULIN COURT

GARDEN CLOISTER

VIEW FROM DIRECTOR'S WINDOW

VIEW OF CHERRY ESPLANADE FROM FIFTH FLOOR BRIDGE

PERSPECTIVE VIEWS

THE BROOKLYN MUSEUM MASTER PLAN COMPETITION

DRAWING NO. 11   SEPTEMBER 15, 1986

SKIDMORE, OWINGS & MERRILL • NEW YORK
VITETTA GROUP/STUDIO FOUR

4.33

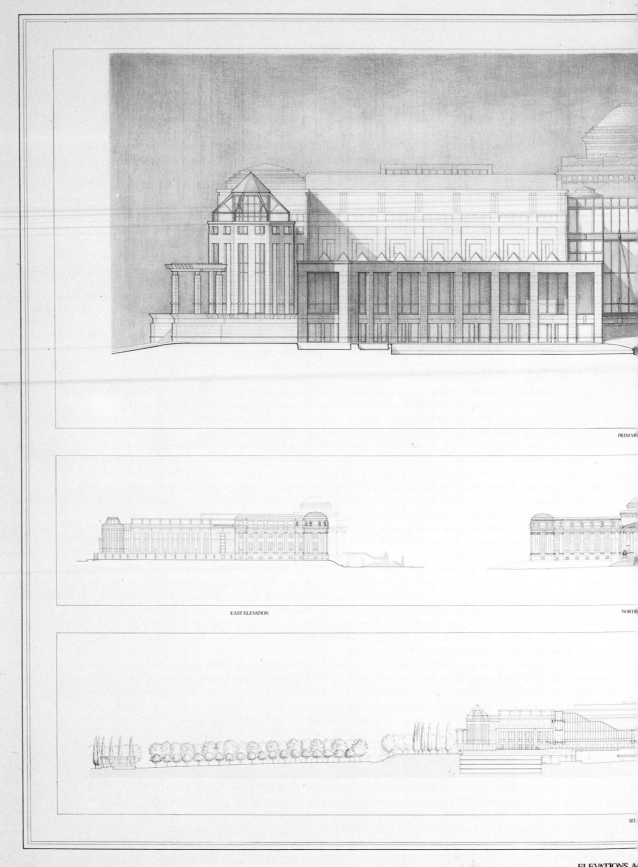

PRIMAR

EAST ELEVATION

NORT

SIT

ELEVATIONS A

THE BROOKLYN MUSEUM

DRAWING NO. 9   DRAWING NO. 10

SKIDMORE, OWINGS &
VITETTA GROU

4.32

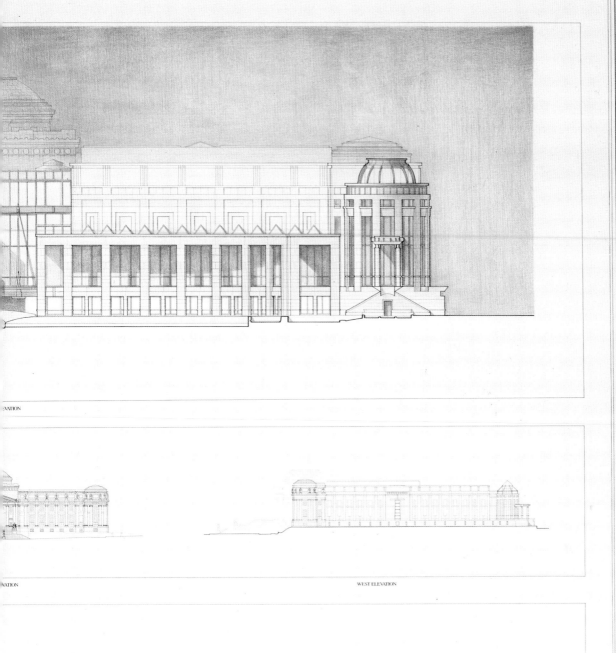

EVATION

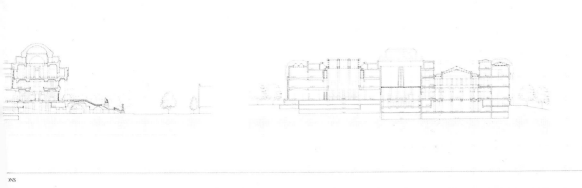

VATION

WEST ELEVATION

NS

ECTIONS

STER PLAN COMPETITION

SEPTEMBER 15, 1986

LL · NEW YORK
O FOUR

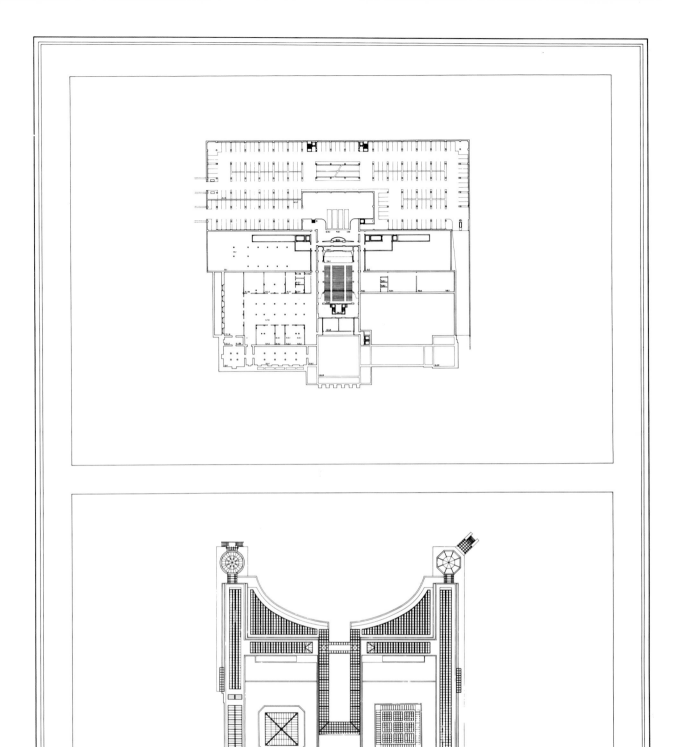

BASEMENT AND ROOF PLANS

THE BROOKLYN MUSEUM MASTER PLAN COMPETITION

DRAWING NO. 8   SEPTEMBER 15, 1986

SKIDMORE, OWINGS & MERRILL • NEW YORK
VITETTA GROUP/STUDIO FOUR

· ARS · LONGA · VITA · BREVIS ·

MUSEUM LOBBY AT PIANO-NOBILE

WEST WING TEMPORARY EXHIBITION GALLERY

VIEW OF RECONSTRUCTED MUSEUM ENTRANCE

EAST WING FIFTH FLOOR GALLERY

PERSPECTIVE VIEWS

THE BROOKLYN MUSEUM MASTER PLAN COMPETITION

DRAWING NO 12   SEPTEMBER 15, 1986

SKIDMORE, OWINGS & MERRILL • NEW YORK
VITETTA GROUP/STUDIO FOUR

141

4.34

Voorsanger & Mills Associates

Team
Bartholomew Voorsanger
Konrad Wos
Kevin Gordon
Anne Perl
David Ling
Satoshi Ohashi
Joseph Sullivan
Knut Hansen
Elizabeth Kamell
Elizabeth Hardwick
Craig Barton
Vicki Smith
Torben Pedersen

Rick Mulder
Michael Kearney
Lewis Jacobsen
Eileen Delgado
Leroy White
Landscape Consultants
Lee Weintraub, Weintraub
  & diDomenico
Cost Estimator
Ray Firman, Hanscomb
  Associates
Presentation Model
Takumi Nishio, Scale
  Images

Richelmo Bottino
Editors
Peggy Healy and Alison
    Freeland, Peggy Healy
    Associates
Catherine Hoover
    Voorsanger

Bartholomew Voorsanger

Bartholomew Voorsanger, FAIA, and Partner in Charge of Design for Voorsanger & Mills Associates, founded the firm with Edward I. Mills, AIA, in September 1978. Mr. Voorsanger received a bachelor's degree in architecture, with honors, from Princeton University in 1960, and a master's degree from Harvard University in 1964. Following his graduation from Harvard, he worked for three years with Vincent Ponte, an urban planner in Montreal. He began working for I. M. Pei & Partners in 1969. As an Associate at I. M. Pei, he was in charge of the firm's overseas work in Iran. Since the inception of Voorsanger & Mills Associates, his work has been published in a wide variety of architectural books and journals in the United States, Europe, and Japan. Some of his major projects include the CBS Theatrical Films Division, Le Cygne Restaurant, the New York Chapter headquarters of the American Institute of Architects, the Neiman Barge House, New York University dormitories, and the New York University School for Continuing Education.

Mr. Voorsanger's work has been exhibited at The Museum of Architecture in Finland, The Architectural Association in London, Harvard University's Graduate School of Design, The Hudson River Museum, New York University, and Rice University. He has served on design-award juries for several major national publications and a number of regional and national architectural organizations. Featured speaker at numerous design symposia, he has authored articles for architectural and art periodicals. Mr. Voorsanger has been a guest lecturer and critic and has taught architectural studies at the Rhode Island School of Design (where he is on the Visiting Committee for the School of Architecture), Columbia, Harvard, and the University of Pennsylvania. He served on the Board of Directors of the New York Chapter of the American Institute of Architects and is currently Chairman of its Gallery Exhibition Committee.

Konrad Wos, Senior Associate at Voorsanger & Mills Associates, joined the firm in 1980. He received his bachelor's degree in architecture from Cornell University in 1975 and his master's degree in architecture from Princeton University in 1977. He holds a diploma in real estate finance and investment analysis from New York University's School of Continuing Education. Mr. Wos has lectured at The Architectural Association of London and Kingston Polytechnic as an associate professor and critic and has also served as visiting critic at Yale, Columbia, and Syracuse universities. He has been initial project architect for La Grandeur Condominiums in Phoenix and project architect for the Loeb & Loeb law offices and the Cardini Restaurant in Los Angeles and for the Manhattan Transfer video-editing studios, San Paolo Bank, and the CBS Theatrical Films Division in New York.

Kevin Gordon, Associate at Voorsanger & Mills Associates, has been a project designer with the firm since 1984. He received his master's degree in architecture and his bachelor's degree in environmental design from Miami University in Ohio. Mr. Gordon has taught at the University of Cincinnati and Miami University and has received awards in AIA competitions. He was project architect on the Barge House and New York University dormitories. He is a registered architect in New York and Ohio and a member of the NCARB.

Lee Weintraub is a principal in the landscape-architecture firm of Weintraub & diDomenico. He received his bachelor's degree in urban landscape at City College of New York and is a registered landscape architect in New York. Mr. Weintraub has been the principal planner for the Department of Planning and Development in Trenton, New Jersey, and a landscape architect for the Department of Housing, Preservation & Development in New York City. He has designed many parks, including Tiffany Plaza, Charlton Parks, Academy Courts, and the Longfellow Gardens in the Bronx; Bayview Park in Coney Island; and the East Harlem Art Park. He has taught landscape design at City College of New York and has been a visiting critic at Harvard University's Graduate School of Design.

145

Project Description

The architectural competition as a format for the significant exploration of credible ideas bears rewards for both benefactor and participant. For the latter, the competition offers a departure from the daily distractions of practice. For the former, it places the individual or institution in the position of patron-of-the-moment on the cutting edge of ongoing architectural debate. Such patronage by a cultural institution can be a tonic, infusing new vigor into worn perceptions, both public and private. It was our hope that by producing a true master-plan strategy, one of discrete, formally autonomous additions over time, we could ensure that The Brooklyn Museum would align itself with the changing faces of the avant-garde well into the next century.

In our opinion, phased construction is the most important formal component of the Museum's program, which calls for the addition of approximately 500,000 square feet of galleries, offices, storage, and public-support facilities— virtually doubling the size of the Museum—in increments of approximately $20 million. (The Museum did not define its priorities beyond the first phase, which includes the reconstruction of the Grand Staircase on Eastern Parkway and the restoration of the West Wing.)

Given the real challenge of fund raising on such a large scale, we felt that probably only two or three phases of new construction would be completed within the next two decades. Therefore, rather than designing a ''complete'' building we chose instead to evolve an architectural ''strategy'' or master plan. We resolved to make each of the five new construction phases a self-contained fundable element hinged to a new spatial armature connecting the Museum with its garden context. Such a plan is eminently fundable because each phase would be a formally autonomous fragment comprising a slice of the Museum's total program of coherent circulation, new galleries, offices, storage, and support space. Formally independent at each stage, the Museum would function with or without the completion of the master plan. Furthermore, each phase presents a different, identifiable metaphor in relation to the Museum precinct and Botanic Garden, yet the master plan is ultimately driven by the wish for the completed phases to frame a new monumental space. Ironically, in part the goal of fund raising would be the formation of the intangible, memorable exterior space standing in relation to the Museum, the Botanic Garden, and the Atlantic Basin beyond.

The essence of a truly successful master plan is its flexibility—allowing different architects to design individual elements without being bound by one stylistic point of view, while being unified by a formal architectural strategy so compelling that it warrants completion. Our master plan is predicated on the notion of the building as connected fragments, in this case the building as a cluster of fragments, a pinwheel of thin sections in the amorphous confines of the plinthlike Museum precinct, yet defining a single figured space in reciprocity with the space of the Cherry Esplanade in the Botanic Garden. The circulation routes are always on the periphery of the building, so that the visitor is oriented by definitive exterior space and a clear view of the building and the surrounding gardens. (Progression in the existing building is so interrupted that the great internal spaces, instead of being exciting destinations, are often never found. The frustration of the infrequent visitor perpetually lost in the Museum distracts and distances the visitor from the art.) One strength of our strategy is that the order in which additions are made can be altered, and future additions can logically continue beyond the present program. This Modernist solution is actually suggested by the existing Museum, itself an architectural fragment, though Classical in style. In our view, the most respectful treatment of this building is a master plan that neither emulates nor reinterprets the original design but reveals the inherent beauty of its interior spaces and integrates building and landscape.

The Museum at present represents less than one-quarter of the building envisioned by McKim, Mead & White, a grand four-square, Beaux-Arts scheme with a circulation armature in the center. It consists of only one square, one perimeter wing, and one complete facade. Like a Potemkin village, the Museum's south facade facing the Botanic Garden is raw and unfinished. Although McKim, Mead & White presented their scheme as a master plan, one that could be constructed in stages, it was not a master plan at all. It was a *building* that required completion in order to function successfully. Without perpendicular circulation spines in the center, the four squares and four facades were destined to become dead ends and, as is presently the case, galleries were forced into service as areas for passage and storage as well as for display. Conversely, if first the cruciform circulation system had been built, unfinished interior walls would have become exterior walls until the four squares and the four facades were in place.

Even in its limited greatness, however, The Brooklyn Museum as it now stands boasts superb architectural elements that our master plan celebrates anew: the Classical facade and two magnificent internal spaces—the third-floor Beaux-Arts Court and the fifth-floor Rotunda. We conceive of the main entrance, facing Eastern Parkway, as an urban plaza adorned with parallel rows of cherry trees and symmetrical reflecting pools, serving both the Museum and the Botanic Garden. A new Grand Staircase reestablishes and makes accessible the Piano Nobile (third floor) as the main public entrance to the Museum. We ventilated the relentless horizontality of the original building by cutting an opening in the fourth and fifth floors above the third-floor entrance, thus maximizing the drama of the Rotunda and creating a spectacular vertical vista, 120 feet high, into its dome. The Beaux-Arts Court, for so long a hermetic space, now opens into a glazed reception court added to the Piano Nobile in the second phase of construction. This monumental, five-

147

story, light-filled space resolves for the first time the north-south axis of the Museum, established by the main entrance, and the east-west axis, established by the Beaux-Arts Court. It is a crossroads within the Museum. From here the visitor can exit south toward the Botanic Garden, turn east to the Beaux-Arts Court, north to the main entrance, or west to the new West Wing added in the second phase. The reception court performs an exterior function as well, healing the unfinished south facade and providing the main entrance to the Museum from the Botanic Garden.

The Museum's site relationship to the Botanic Garden was left unresolved along with the unfinished McKim, Mead & White building. Had it been completed, McKim, Mead & White's Museum would have been integrated with the landscape. The Olmsted Brothers anticipated this relationship by planting double rows of cherry trees in an esplanade perpendicular to the Museum's south facade. In the absence of any physical or conceptual connection to the building, however, the Cherry Esplanade appears absurdly isolated, leading nowhere. In fact, the Museum is currently separated from landscape gardens on two sides. A large parking lot and Washington Avenue surround the building like a moat, cutting it off from the Botanic Garden to the south and Guider Park to the east, while the truncated West Wing of the original Museum ends abruptly without so much as a gesture toward the Osborne Terrace. The vacant mid-ground between Museum and landscape is a sensitive area that poses important conceptual questions: How should it be occupied? Formally or informally? By building or by nature? Now, or in future decades?

The new wing we propose in the first phase of construction is critical to the resolution of this issue. Metaphorically, it is a drawbridge spanning the parking lot to the Botanic Garden, with a gentle cascade of exterior stairs descending gradually from the fifth floor of the Museum (with entrances to the building on every floor) to a crescent-shaped berm thirty feet high at the level of the Museum's second floor overlooking the Cherry Esplanade. The waterfall fountain flanked by stairs added in the second phase mediates between the Museum and the Garden while preserving the overlook to the lawns and gardens below.

This wing, typical of each addition in the master plan, contains a cross section of new spaces the Museum requires. It houses new storage (basement level), African, Oceanic, and New World art galleries and education facilities (first floor), Egyptian art galleries (second floor), double-height changing exhibition galleries (third floor), decorative-arts galleries (fourth floor), a public restaurant with spectacular views of the Botanic Garden and the city (fifth floor), and executive administrative offices with equally breathtaking vistas (sixth floor). (There are virtually no views of the Garden or to the west from the existing building.)

Shallow parterres adjacent to this wing extend by 400 feet the axis established by the Cherry Esplanade, ascending from the Garden berm to the glazed reception court at the Piano Nobile level. When a parallel wing is added in the third construction phase, the extended Esplanade is transformed into a monumental terraced courtyard enclosed on three sides, an external gallery for sculpture and summer concerts nearly the width of Park Avenue in New York and similar in spatial intensity to the Uffizi Gallery in Florence. The Museum would now have for the first time an external court, a spatial dividend of the constructed master plan that would serve as a counterpoint to its magnificent internal galleries.

In our fourth phase of construction we annex Guider Park to both the Botanic Garden and the Museum. Guider Park, a triangular island severed from both institutions by Washington Avenue, is currently unclaimed by the urban fabric, the Museum precinct, or the landscape. Washington Avenue, a through street, is not a major thoroughfare, and traffic can be rerouted, as it is on Broadway at Seventy-second Street in New York. With the assimilation of Guider Park, the Museum would at last be situated on a site commensurate with its grand size and flanked on three sides by the Garden, which itself would be enhanced by greater contact with Eastern Parkway.

The park is designated jointly as an extension of the Botanic Garden and the Museum precinct to be used as a children's garden and an area in which to display the Museum's collection of architectural artifacts. The existing lake in the Botanic Garden is extended within this landscape. A new vehicular and pedestrian bridge spans the lake from Washington Avenue and arrives at a semicircular drive in front of a new education wing that subsumes the existing service wing built in the 1970s. This wing encloses the community entrance with an architectural porch that joins the new children's garden and the education wing.

The fifth and last phase of construction completes the Museum's support facilities with underground parking for a thousand automobiles and connects the west wings with a gently curved plinth that meets the Osborne Terrace and mediates the boundaries of garden and architecture, integrating landscape and building.

In the next century, the new architecture of the Museum must respond to the intensity of renewed community interest and the renaissance of its urban neighbors. After a century of estrangement, it should consummate a marriage to the Botanic Garden and exhilarate visitors with the splendor of its new interior, a setting for the avant-garde and the historic. The legacy of The Brooklyn Museum is one of extraordinary scholarship and world-renowned collections. This architectural expansion will rekindle public interest, encourage increased participation, and create a new and dynamic identity.

149

4.37

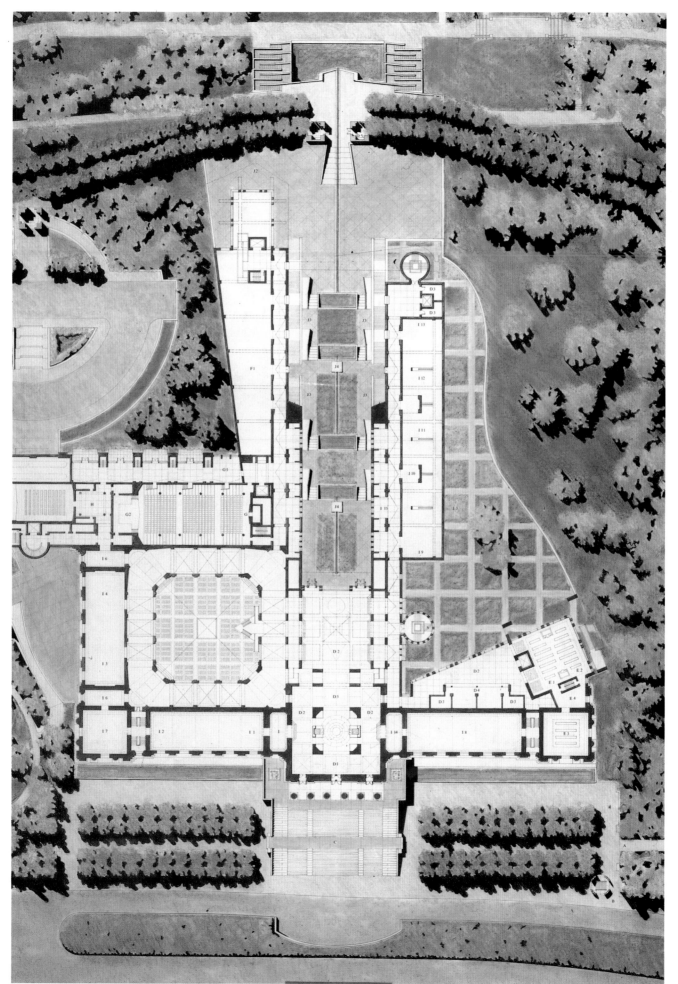

4.38

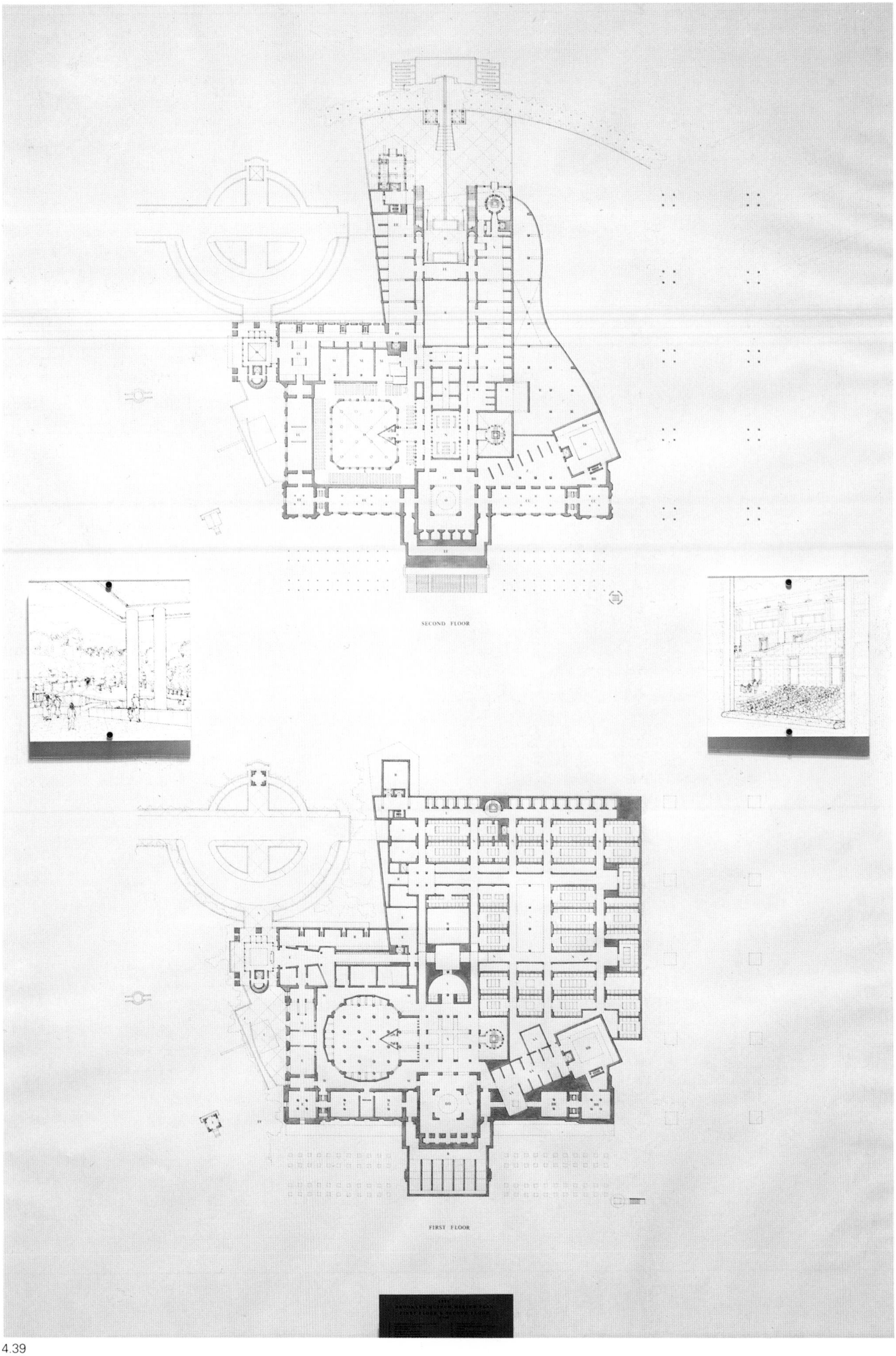

SECOND FLOOR

FIRST FLOOR

154

4.39

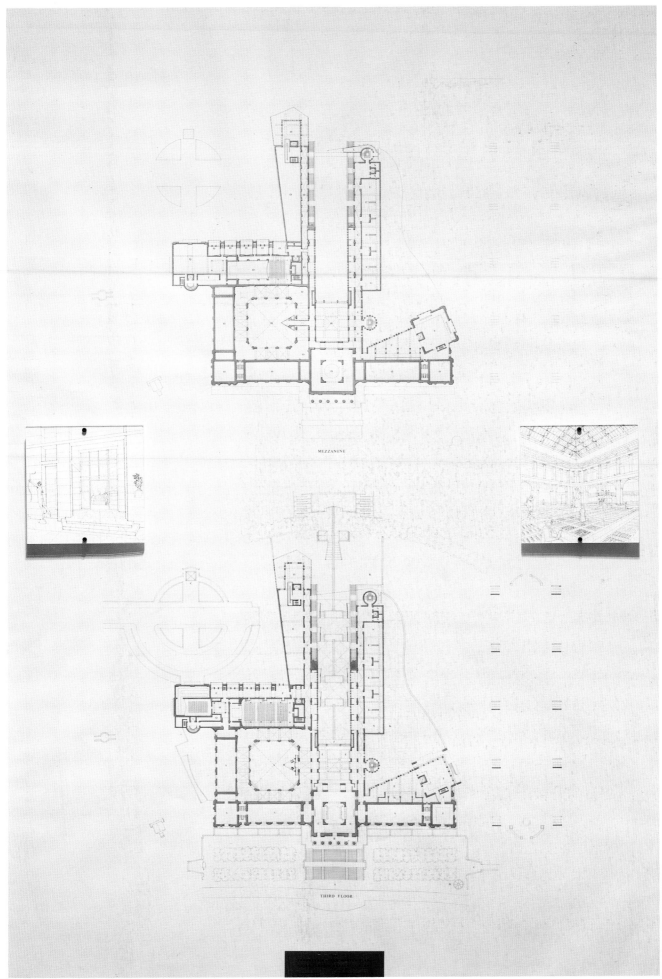

MEZZANINE

THIRD FLOOR

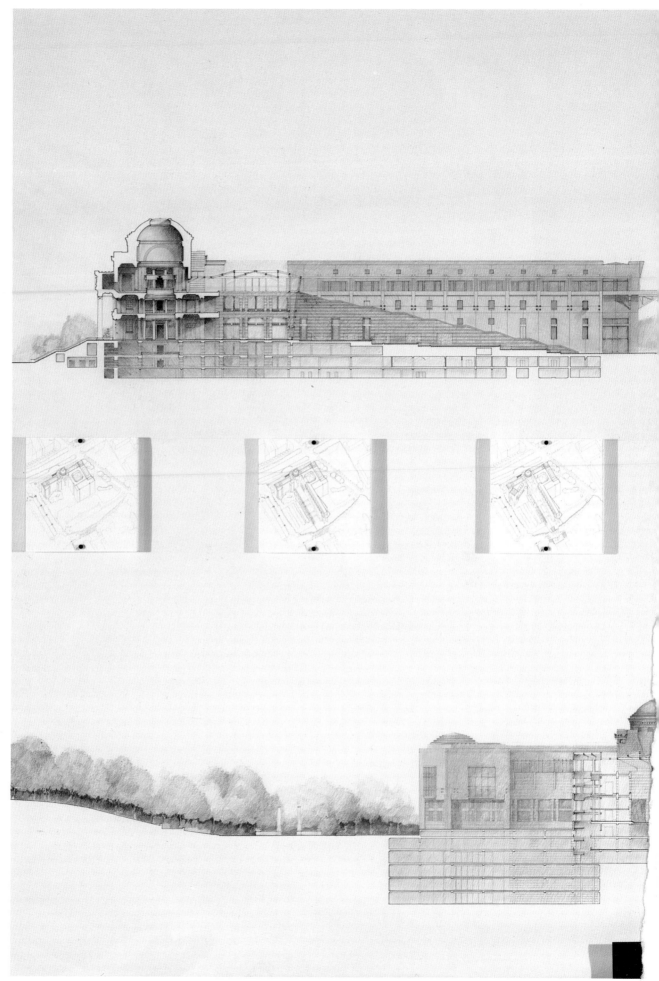

4.43

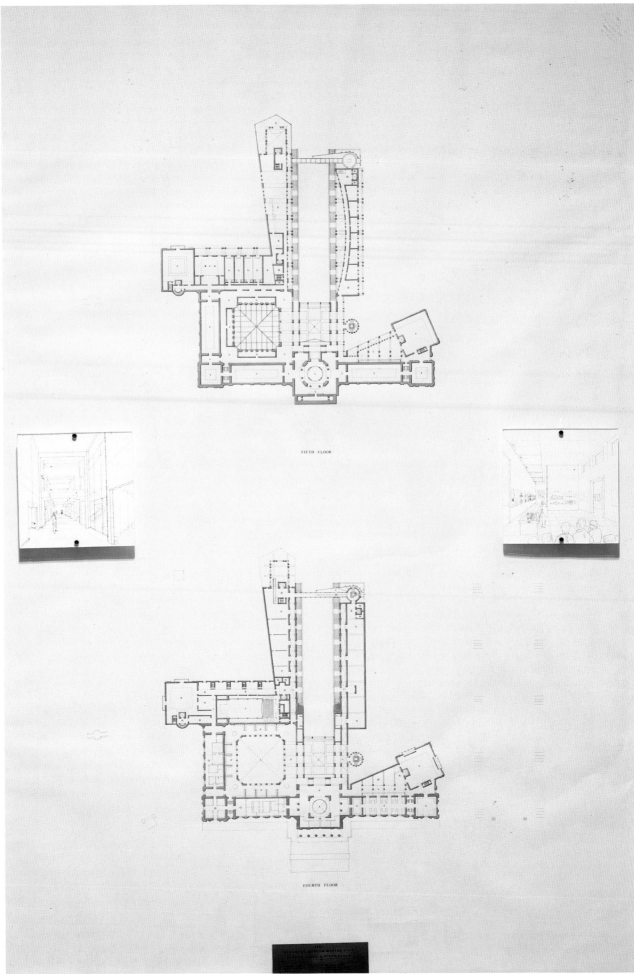

FIFTH FLOOR

FOURTH FLOOR

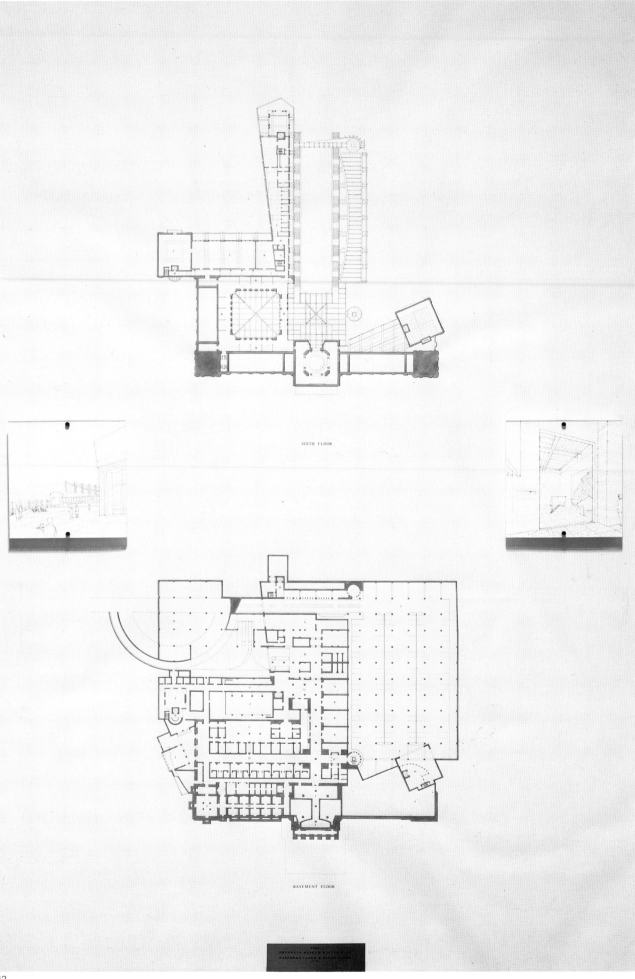

SIXTH FLOOR

BASEMENT FLOOR

4.42

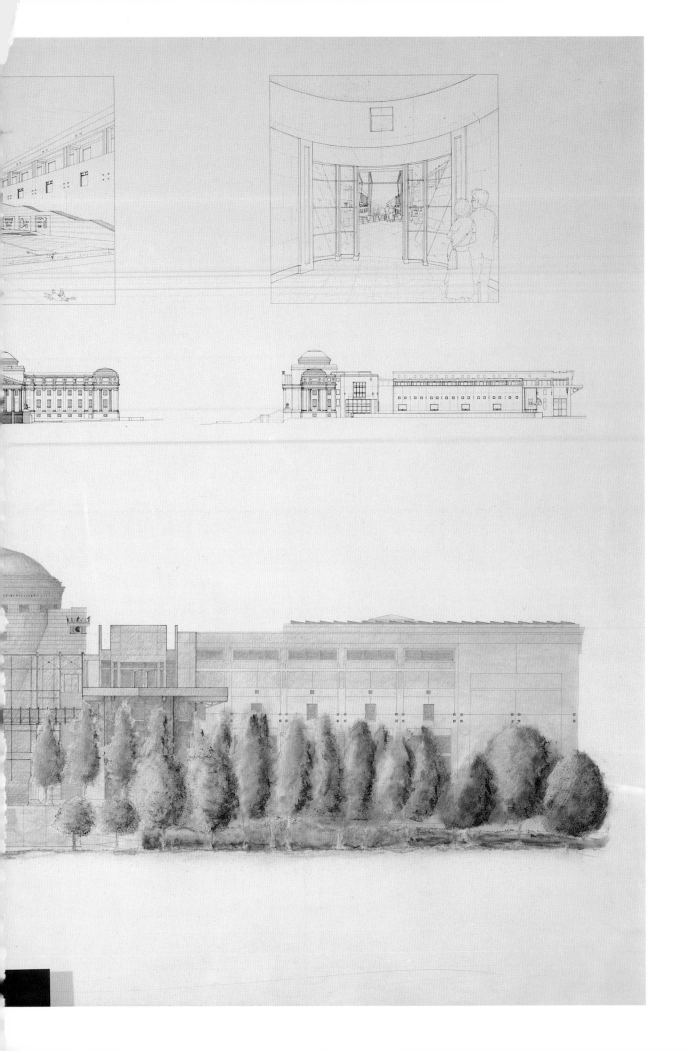

4.44

4.45

Award of the Jury

Award of the Jury

Arata Isozaki & Associates/
James Stewart Polshek and Partners

Teams
Arata Isozaki
James Stewart Polshek
Isozaki Team
Makoto Shin Watanabe
Hiroshi Jun Aoki
Yusaku Imamura
Fumio Matsumoto
Polshek Team
Duncan Hazard
James Garrison
David Bylund
Kurt Carlson

Uday Dhar
Blake Middleton
Ron Milewicz
David Sherman
Special Coordinator
Ann Kaufman
Model Maker
Shoji Ishiguro,
    Ishiguro Model Inc.
Silkscreen Printer
Ryo'ichi Ishida
Renderings
Lebbeus Woods

4:46

Graphic-Design Consultant
Ann Harakawa,
    Ann Harakawa, Inc.
Structural-Engineering
    Consultant
Robert Silman,
    Robert Silman
    Associates
Mechanical-Electrical
    Engineering Consultants
Goldman Sokolow
    Copeland, P.C.
Thomas A. Polise C.E.

Arata Isozaki

James Stewart Polshek

Arata Isozaki & Associates was founded by Mr. Isozaki in 1963. His work is internationally known and includes numerous museums and civic buildings. A partial listing of the works he has completed in the last decade includes the Gunma Prefectural Museum of Fine Arts, the Kitakyushu City Museum of Art, the Fujimi Country Clubhouse, the Kitakyushu City Central Library, the Kamioka Town Hall, the Audio-Visual Center of Oita City, the Wasada Sho-gekijo Toga Sanbo Theater, the Museum of Contemporary Art in Los Angeles, the Tsukuba Center Building, the Palladium in New York, the Okanoyama Graphic Art Museum, the Iwata High School Complex, and the Annex of the Kitakyushu City Museum of Art. His projects in progress include the Sports Hall for the 1992 Olympics in Barcelona, the Shufu-no-tomo Cultural Complex, the Tokyo University of Art and Design, and the National Museum of Egyptian Civilization, Cairo. Mr. Isozaki is an Honorary Fellow of Academia Tiberina, the American Institute of Architects, and the Bund Deutscher Architekten. He is a recipient of the Gold Medal for Architects from the Royal Institute of British Architects.

James Stewart Polshek, FAIA, is Senior Partner and founder of James Stewart Polshek and Partners. He is a graduate of Case Western Reserve and Yale universities and completed his postgraduate studies as a Fulbright Scholar at the Royal Academy of Fine Arts in Copenhagen. Mr. Polshek began the independent practice of architecture in 1963 and from 1972 to June 1987 was Dean of the Columbia University Graduate School of Architecture, Planning and Preservation. His significant work of the last decade includes 500 Park Tower, an addition to the Pepsi-Cola building in New York; the Rochester Riverside Convention Center in Rochester, New York; the U.S. Embassy in the Sultanate of Oman; Glenfield Middle School in Montclair, New Jersey; Stroh River Place in Detroit; the Urban Center in New York; the New York Society Library; the Brooklyn Academy of Music;

Carnegie Hall; and Boston Symphony Hall. Mr. Polshek's designs have received numerous awards, including two Honor Awards from the American Institute of Architects in 1972, seven Architectural Design Citations and awards from *Progressive Architecture,* and two New York City AIA Distinguished Architecture Awards in 1985. In 1986 Mr. Polshek received the New York AIA Medal of Honor.

Hiroshi Jun Aoki received a bachelor of architecture degree from the University of Tokyo. At Arata Isozaki & Associates, he has worked as the project designer on the Iwata High School Complex, the Phoenix Municipal Government Center Competition, and the Tokyo City Hall Competition, among numerous other projects. Mr. Aoki is a registered architect in Japan.

Makoto Shin Watanabe received bachelor's and master's degrees in architecture from Kyoto University. He also holds a master's degree in architecture from the Graduate School of Design at Harvard University. At Arata Isozaki & Associates, he has worked as the project designer of the Museum of Contemporary Art in Los Angeles, the Palladium in New York, and the Suffolk County Courthouse Competition.

James Garrison joined James Stewart Polshek and Partners in 1977 and since then has assumed a principal design role on many projects, including the Rochester Riverside Convention Center in Rochester, New York; Glenfield Middle School in Montclair, New Jersey; 500 Park Tower in New York; the U.S. Consulate in Lyons; and the U.S. Embassy in the Sultanate of Oman, all of which have received Citation of Design Excellence awards from *Progressive Architecture.* Mr. Garrison is a graduate of Syracuse University.

Duncan Hazard joined James Stewart Polshek and Partners in 1980 and has assumed a principal management role on

many projects, including the IBM National Accounts Division Headquarters in White Plains, New York; the Dillon Read & Co. corporate headquarters in New York; and the U.S. Embassy in the Sultanate of Oman. He is an honors graduate of Yale University and the Columbia University Graduate School of Architecture, Planning and Preservation.

Project Description

The original master plan for The Brooklyn Institute of Arts and Sciences by McKim, Mead & White was created in the Beaux-Arts style, which achieved grandeur and sublimity through the rigorous and systematic application of the architectural language of Classicism. Although conceived nearly a century ago, the original plan has been only partially realized.

Evolution. In preparing our proposal for the new master plan for the Museum, we began by carefully and respectfully analyzing the original McKim, Mead & White design, seeking to discover within its framework intrinsic principles from which our new plan might evolve. In so doing, we have sought to create a monument not to the *synthesis* of old and new architecture but to the *evolution* of a new architecture from the old—an architecture of the twenty-first century derived from that of the nineteenth. The principles that we uncovered in our search and used to guide this evolution are as follows:

The Orders. The Five Architectural Orders of Vignola—Doric, Ionic, Corinthian, Composite, and Tuscan—constitute the basic vocabulary of the Beaux-Arts style. These Orders came into being one by one, each at a given time over a long period of history. They were well established as the basic language of architecture by Roman times and were reconfirmed during the Renaissance.

If the Orders constitute the vocabulary of Classical architecture, the *ordering principles* of scale, proportion, tectonics, and surface characteristics, among others, constitute its syntax. While modern architecture, as it developed in this century, is generally thought to have totally rejected Classicism by eliminating all of the Orders from building design, it continued to depend on those intrinsic syntactic ordering principles that have been common to all architecture from the dawn of history. The frame and the infill (or grid) panel have become the modern Orders, and their surface expression no longer depends only on relief or plasticity but also on smoothness—the flush surface. Thus, as contemporary evolutions of the Classical Orders, we recognize the modern:
•Frame
 and
•Infill Panel

In our design proposal, these "Contemporary Orders," applied to the new portions of the Museum, are juxtaposed with the Classical Orders of the existing Museum building, the proportions and dimensions of the new being derived directly from the old. The frame and infill panel are employed for both the interior and exterior finishes of the new construction. On the new West Wing gallery and south facades, flush-detailed limestone frames infilled with sandblasted stainless steel and glass panels echo the proportions and continue the regulating lines of the existing building's majestic Classical facade. The sleek titanium panels cladding the rotated pavilions at the southwest and southeast corners of the Museum complex serve as foils to the more traditional materials of the existing building and new West Wing. The gridded limestone panels and ceiling coffers facing the walls and ceilings of the monumental interior spaces, the Central and Great Halls, also echo the design and materials of the original design.

Composition. The original Beaux-Arts plan by McKim, Mead & White is based on a perfect square with a clear tripartite facade composed of a central pavilion with two wings that visually reinforce the intended hierarchy of the building's center. The elements of its volumetric composition are cubes, spheres, and cylinders applied repeatedly at different scales according to their hierarchical location relative to the center.

The major volumes of the new addition are set on a plinth that raises the principal public spaces to the level of the Piano Nobile as determined by the original design. These new volumes are designed not to exceed the framework of scale set by McKim, Mead & White. The pavilionlike, cubical element at the southwest corner and the eastern apse, with its domed half-cylinder shape at the center of the east facade, are literal reproductions of elements from the original design. The new gallery wings between these elements maintain the cornice height of the existing building. And the vaulted ceiling of the Central Hall, whose southern end forms the entry porch of the Botanic Garden facade, conforms in form and dimension to that of the original design.

Above the Great Hall, at the center of the Museum circulation system, rises an obelisk, 150 feet in height. Designed to recall the unbuilt central dome that, as envisioned by McKim, Mead & White, would have risen 250 feet above the Piano Nobile level, the obelisk will stand as the visual symbol, thematic center, and generator of circulation for the

169

new Museum. Clad in limestone both inside and out, indirectly lit by a sun-controlled skylight at its top, the Great Hall is intended to house the constantly changing collections of the pivotal Curator's Choice galleries, which offer a foretaste of the rich collections housed in the galleries that surround this central volume.

Formal Manipulation. In our design proposal, three degrees of formal manipulation—Reproduction, Rotation, and Allusion—are used to reinforce the previously discussed devices of Order and Composition in the evolution and extension of the original McKim, Mead & White design.

Reproduction: The literal reproduction of original design elements, including the southwest pavilion and eastern apse referred to above, as well as the careful restorations of the Beaux-Arts Court, Piano Nobile Lobby, and fifth-floor Rotunda, and the reconstruction of the original, monumental North Entry Stair, creates keystone elements for the recollection of the original design within the fabric of the new total building organization. For these keystone pieces, the reproduction of form is reinforced by a careful duplication of original materials, including the exterior limestone cladding and interior flooring, wall, and ceiling materials.

Rotation: To the governing north-south and east-west axes of the original McKim, Mead & White plan, a new axis, parallel to Washington Avenue, has been added. The southeast wing containing the Museum's new dining facilities with their open-air sculpture/dining terrace has been rotated to meet this new axis, creating a generous and inviting forecourt opening to the Brooklyn Botanic Garden to the south of the Museum complex. This new axial relationship to the edge of the Botanic Garden will complement the traditional relationship of the Museum's central axis to the Garden's Cherry Esplanade, which has been strengthened in the new design by the extension of the south Piano Nobile terrace to the edge of the Garden's existing berm and by our suggestion for the construction of a new monumental ramping system within the Garden's property to make the transition from the Piano Nobile to the lower level of the Esplanade lawn.

The circulation bridges along the south face of the new trapezoidal Rodin Court are orthogonal to this new axis, recalling the orientation of the new southeast wing while engaging the Botanic Garden to the west by extending through the new West Wing, to connect by means of a terrace and bridge, to the Garden's Osborne Terrace and the new "reservoir" and amphitheater complex beyond. This new outdoor performance space, with its restored reservoir replacing the existing man-made Mount Prospect Park, will, by its orthogonal relationship to the axis of Washington Avenue, knit the Museum's relationship to the Botanic Garden on both its south and west sides, while improving visual access to the Museum and Garden from Grand Army Plaza and providing, with the "backdrop" of the new West Wing, a truly grand open-air performance space appropriate to this center of cultural life for Brooklyn.

To the east of the Museum, the same new axis will be further reinforced by the orthogonal orientation of the east entrance walkway and the alignment with this walkway of the new entrance to Guider Park across Washington Avenue. Within the Museum, the new outdoor sculpture court, adjacent to the new Museum dining facility and parallel to the Washington Avenue axis, forms a "rotated" complement to the restored Beaux-Arts Court.

Allusion: Within the fabric of the new Museum, allusions to the plan and decorative features of the original McKim, Mead & White design reinforce recollections of the nineteenth century and its continuity with the twenty-first century. The paving pattern of the southern Piano Nobile terrace will duplicate in black-and-white stone that area of the original plan. In the interior design of the public galleries, both new and—where literal restoration is not feasible—old, traditional proportions, materials, and features such as base, cornice, and door and window surrounds will be employed to allude to, without imitating, the interior features of the original Beaux-Arts design.

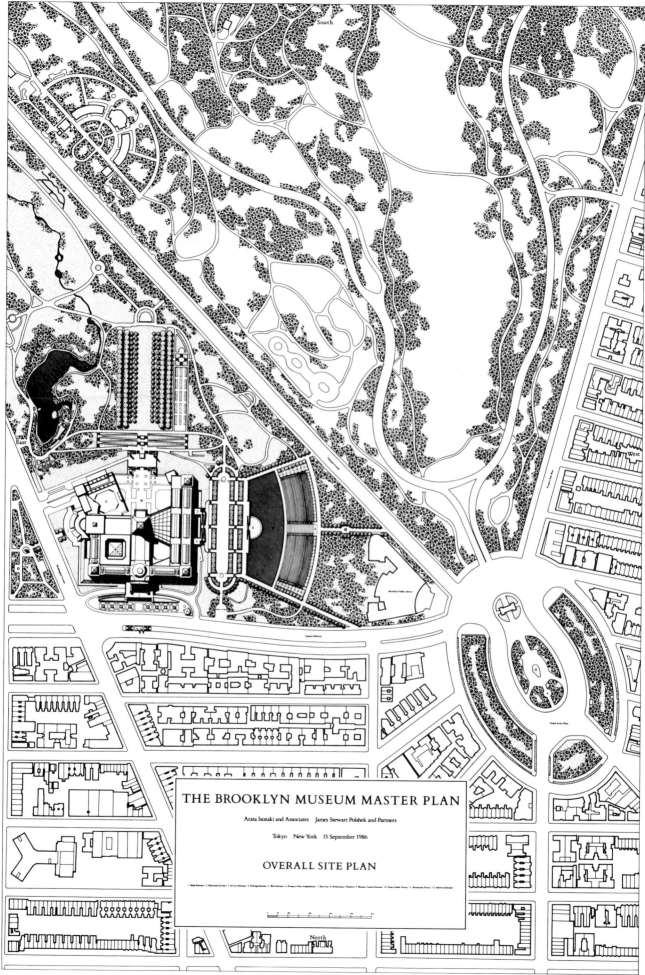

THE BROOKLYN MUSEUM MASTER PLAN

Arata Isozaki and Associates   James Stewart Polshek and Partners

Tokyo   New York   15 September 1986

OVERALL SITE PLAN

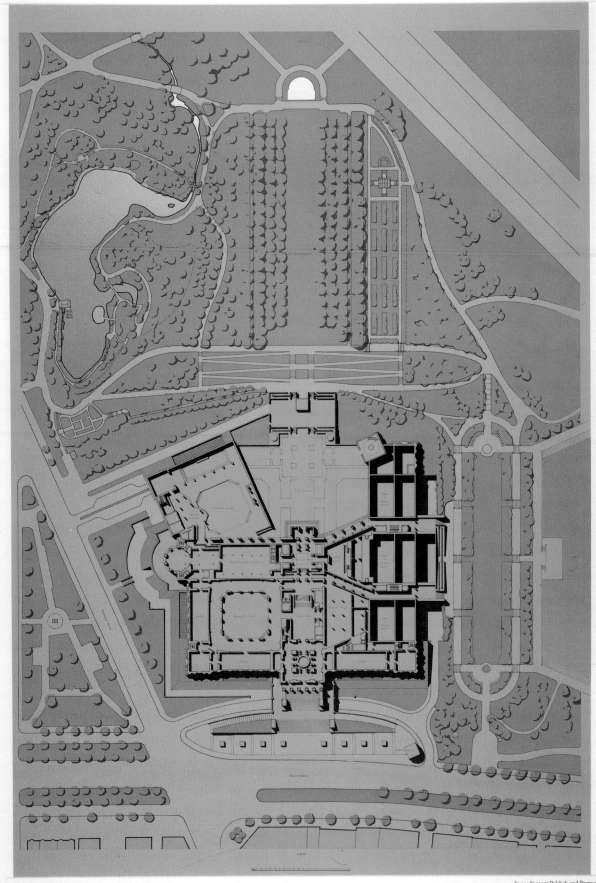

SITE PLAN
THE BROOKLYN MUSEUM MASTER PLAN

NO. 2

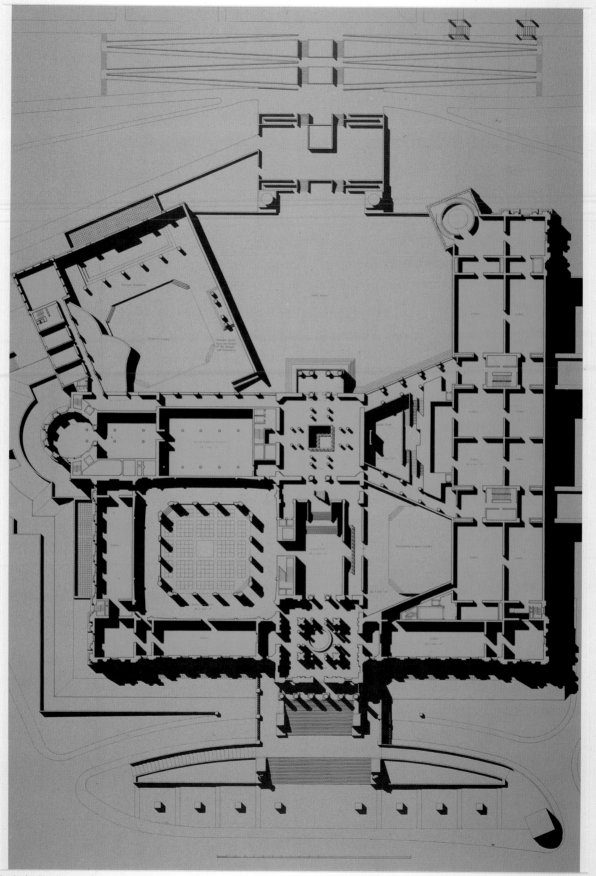

PIANO NOBILE PLAN
THE BROOKLYN MUSEUM MASTER PLAN

NO. 3

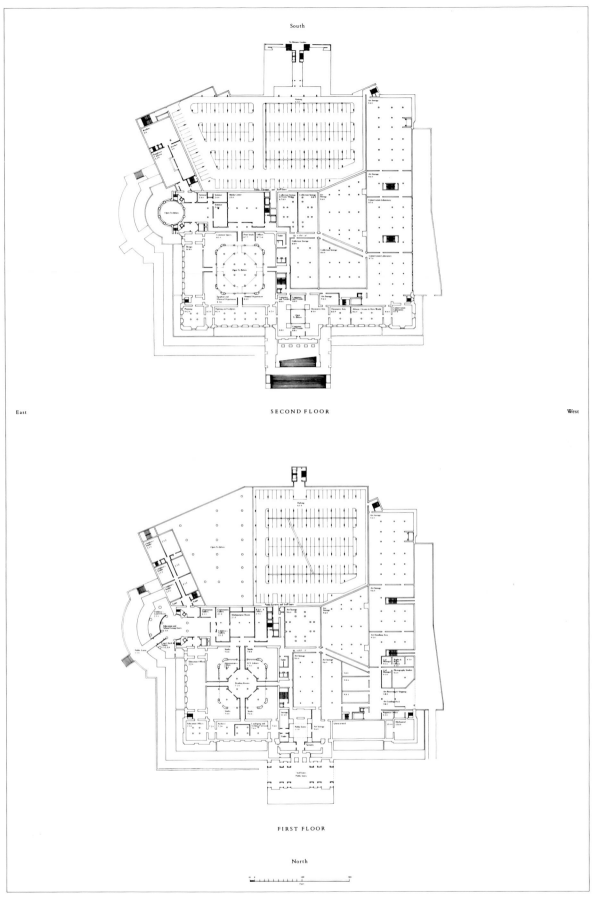

South

SECOND FLOOR

East

West

FIRST FLOOR

North

Arata Isozaki and Associates

James Stewart Polshek and Partners

FLOOR PLAN

THE BROOKLYN MUSEUM MASTER PLAN

NO. 4

4.50

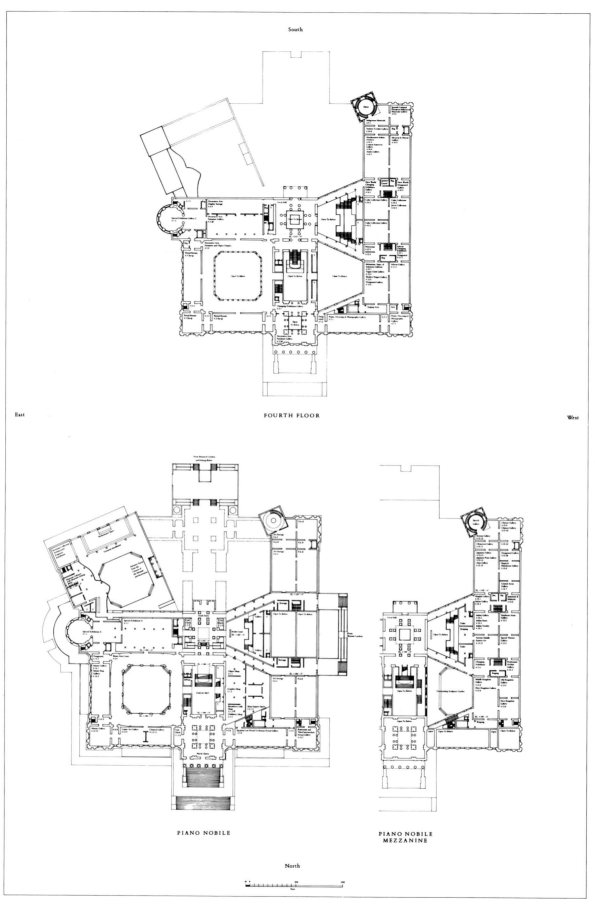

South

FOURTH FLOOR

East

West

PIANO NOBILE

PIANO NOBILE
MEZZANINE

North

Arata Isozaki and Associates

James Stewart Polshek and Partners

FLOOR PLAN

THE BROOKLYN MUSEUM MASTER PLAN

NO. 5

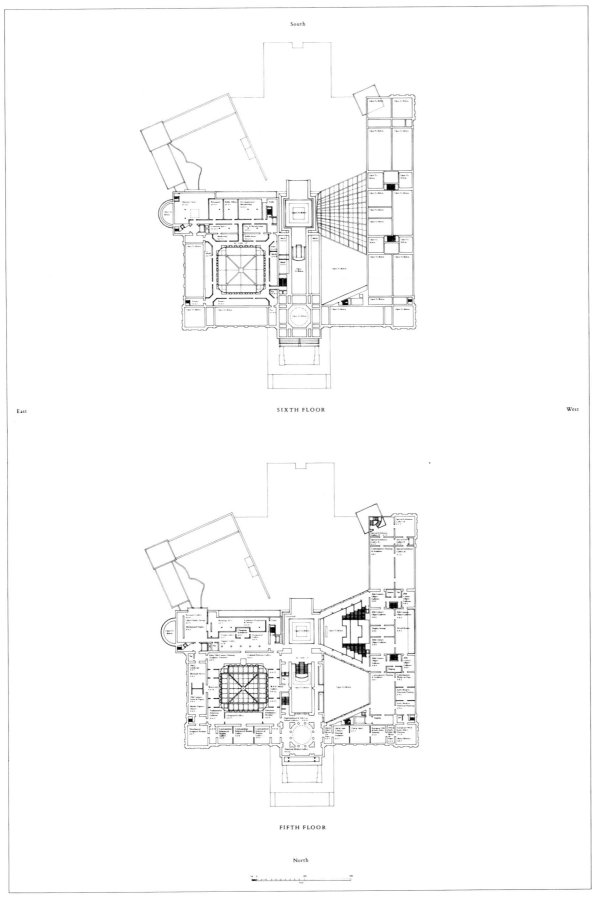

South

SIXTH FLOOR

East   West

FIFTH FLOOR

North

Arata Isozaki and Associates   James Stewart Polshek and Partners

FLOOR PLAN

THE BROOKLYN MUSEUM MASTER PLAN

NO. 6

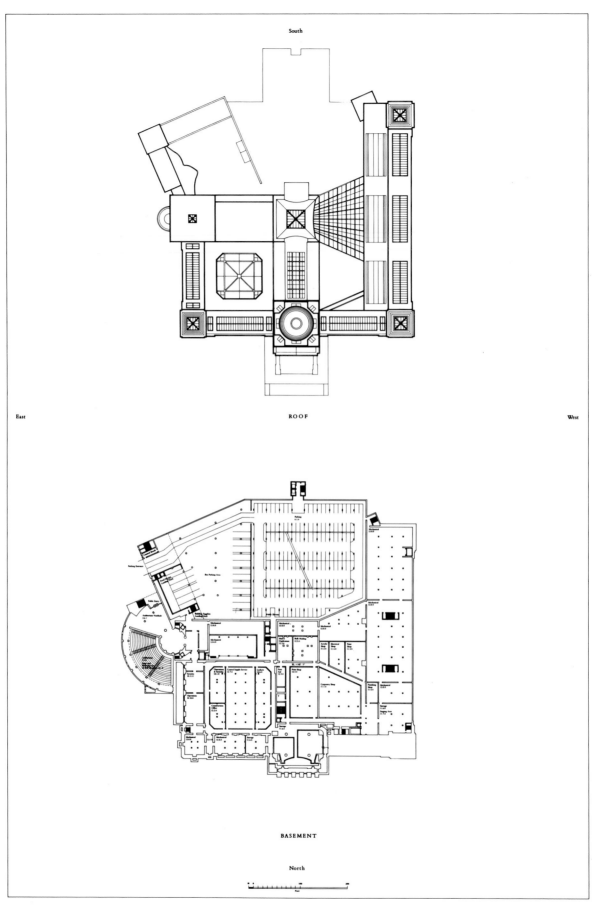

South

East   ROOF   West

BASEMENT

North

Arata Isozaki and Associates   James Stewart Polshek and Partners

FLOOR PLAN

THE BROOKLYN MUSEUM MASTER PLAN

NO. 7

GREAT HALL

RODIN COURT

CENTRAL HALL
From North Entry Hall

Arata Isozaki and Associates

James Stewart Polshek and Partners

PERSPECTIVE VIEWS
THE BROOKLYN MUSEUM MASTER PLAN

NO. 10

Section

Looking West

East-West Section Looking North

East Elevation

South Elevation

James Stewart Polshek and Partners

ELEVATIONS

UM MASTER PLAN

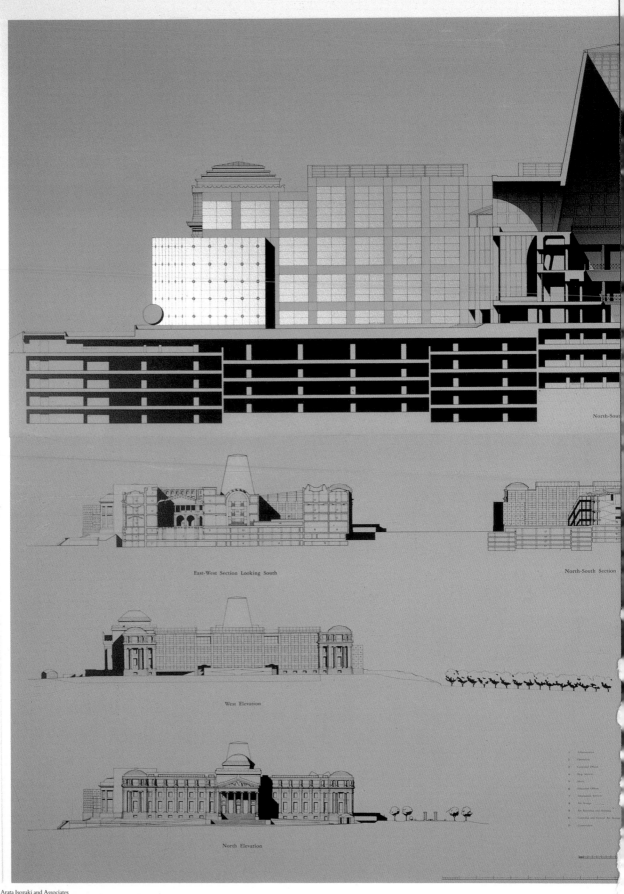

North-South

East-West Section Looking South

North-South Section

West Elevation

North Elevation

Arata Isozaki and Associates

VIEW FROM BOTANIC GARDEN

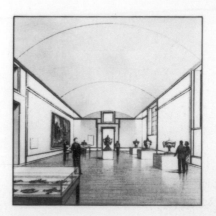

OLD GALLERY

NEW GALLERY

PERSPECTIVE VIEWS

THE BROOKLYN MUSEUM MASTER PLAN

NO. 11

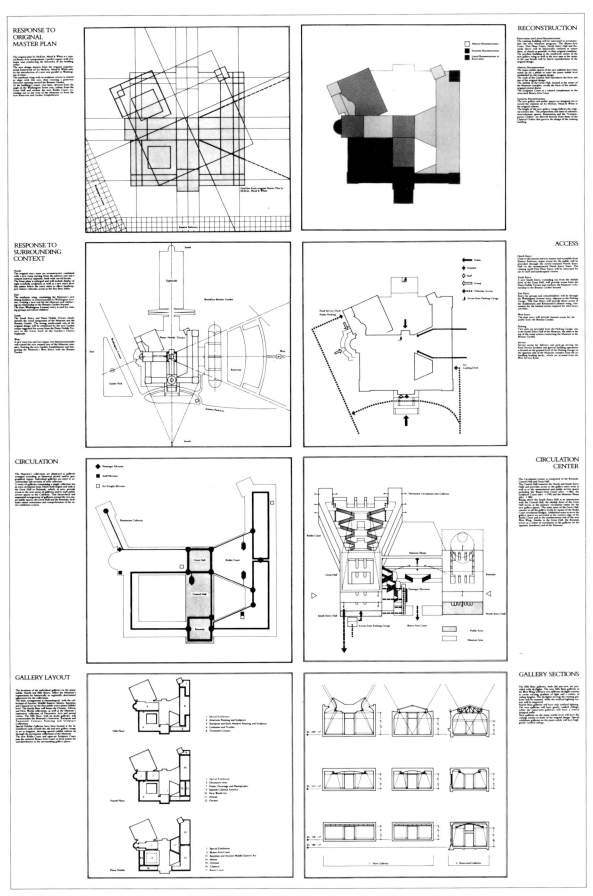

RESPONSE TO ORIGINAL MASTER PLAN

RESPONSE TO SURROUNDING CONTEXT

CIRCULATION

GALLERY LAYOUT

RECONSTRUCTION

ACCESS

CIRCULATION CENTER

GALLERY SECTIONS

Arata Isozaki and Associates

James Stewart Polshek and Partners

DIAGRAMS

THE BROOKLYN MUSEUM MASTER PLAN

NO. 12

184

The Jury on October 8, 1986, in front of the statue of Brooklyn, by Daniel Chester French, at the entrance to The Brooklyn Museum.

5. Jury Report

The Jury

Klaus Herdeg, Chairman of the Jury, is Professor of Architecture at Columbia University, where he was chairman of the Division of Architecture from 1984 to 1986. He received his professional education in Zürich with Werner M. Moser and, after practicing in Zürich and London, studied at Cornell University, receiving a bachelor of architecture degree in 1963, and at Harvard University, earning a master's degree in urban design in 1964. He is a licensed architect and has been teaching design and theory at Cornell and Columbia universities since 1967.

One of Mr. Herdeg's major interests in architecture is the study of the interpretation of universal principles by different cultures. The Eidlitz and Wheelwright fellowships have allowed him to make major research trips to India, Iran, Turkistan, and China, resulting in two traveling exhibitions and publications: *Formal Structure in Indian Architecture,* 1967, and *Formal Structure in Islamic Architecture of Iran and Turkistan,* 1987–88. His 1983 book, *The Decorated Diagram,* dealt with Walter Gropius's term as chairman of the School of Architecture at Harvard. Currently his research is focusing on concession architecture in China in the 1920s and 1930s. Mr. Herdeg has lectured on architecture and been a visiting critic in Europe, China, and the United States.

187

Alastair B. Martin has been on the Board of Trustees of The Brooklyn Museum since 1948 and has served as Chairman since 1984. Mr. Martin was born in New York City and graduated from Princeton University in 1938. He is a Director of the Bessemer Securities Corporation and the Bessemer Group.

Mr. Martin was United States Amateur Court Tennis Singles Champion from 1950 to 1956 and was elected to the National Tennis Hall of Fame in 1973. He served as President of the United States Tennis Association in 1969–70 and as President of the A.S.P.C.A. in 1973–75. He is an honorary trustee of The Metropolitan Museum of Art, New York. With his wife, he formed the Guennol Art Collection, which was exhibited at the Metropolitan Museum in 1970–71; many important objects from the collection are presently on view at The Brooklyn Museum. Before his appointment as Chairman of the Board of Trustees, Mr. Martin was Chairman of the Acquisitions Committee.

Robert S. Rubin was appointed a Trustee of The Brooklyn Institute of Arts and Sciences in 1968. In 1970 he became chairman of the Brooklyn Children's Museum, where he oversaw the completion of the museum's new facility in Brower Park. He has been on the Board of Trustees of The Brooklyn Museum since 1980 and President since 1984.

Mr. Rubin received a bachelor of arts degree from Yale University in 1953 and a master's degree in business administration from Harvard two years later. He served in the U.S. Army Finance Corps from 1955 to 1958 and then joined the securities firm Lehman Brothers, where he became a partner in 1967. Since 1985, he has been an independent financial consultant. In addition to his service as a Trustee of The Brooklyn Museum, he serves on the boards of the Municipal Art Society of New York, St. Ann's School, Polytechnic University, the Brooklyn Children's Museum, the Committee for National Security, and the Brooklyn Hospital/Caledonian Hospital. Mr. Rubin and his family live in Brooklyn Heights.

189

Jeffrey C. Keil has been on the Board of Trustees of The Brooklyn Museum since 1981 and, as Chairman of the Building Committee, served on both the Selection Committee and the Jury for the Master Plan Competition. Mr. Keil graduated from the University of Pennsylvania in 1965 and did graduate work in mathematical statistics at the London School of Economics. He received a master's degree in business administration from Harvard in 1968.

Mr. Keil was an Associate in the Corporate Finance Department at Hayden, Stone Inc. from 1968 to 1970. After that company's merger with Cogan Berlind Weill and Levitt, he became a Second Vice President in 1971 and a Vice President in 1972. He was appointed Senior Vice President of the Corporate Finance Department of Ladenberg, Thalmann and Company in 1972. Mr. Keil joined Republic New York Corporation/Republic National Bank as Executive Vice President and Treasurer in 1973 and is now Vice Chairman of the Bank and President of the Corporation.

Robert T. Buck was appointed Director of The Brooklyn Museum in 1983. A 1961 graduate of Williams College, Mr. Buck received a master of arts degree from the Institute of Fine Arts at New York University, where he wrote his thesis on Géricault's lithographs. He began his professional career as a lecturer and researcher at The Toledo Museum of Art and was appointed assistant curator at the Washington University Gallery of Art in St. Louis in 1965, becoming Director there in 1968. In 1970 he began a long association with the Albright-Knox Art Gallery in Buffalo, first as Assistant Director and then in 1973 as Director.

Mr. Buck has taught at Washington University and the State University of New York at Buffalo. He was a member of the New York Council for the Humanities from 1976 to 1982 and a United States Commissioner for the Venice Biennale in 1978. He served on the Board of Trustees of the Association of Art Museum Directors from 1978 to 1981 and later as Secretary and Second Vice President. Since becoming Director of The Brooklyn Museum, Mr. Buck has overseen the Museum's process of self-examination and renewal, which has resulted in the search for an architect to develop a master plan to take the Museum into the next century.

Phyllis Lambert is Director of the Centre Canadien d'Architecture in Montreal and is active as an architect, critic, and historic conservationist. She attended Vassar College and received a master's degree in architecture from the Illinois Institute of Technology in Chicago. She holds honorary doctorates from The Technical University of Nova Scotia, the Université de Montréal, McGill University, and Concordia University.

Ms. Lambert was the Director of Planning during the conception and construction of the Seagram Building in New York and in 1984 received the American Institute of Architects' Twenty-Five Year Award in recognition of that achievement. Her design for the renovation of the Biltmore Hotel in Los Angeles received the National Honor Award of the American Institute of Architects, and her design for the Saidye Bronfman Centre in Montreal received the Massey Medal of the Royal Architectural Institute of Canada. She is the founding President of the Heritage Montreal Foundation, which is devoted to protecting that city's architectural heritage.

Ms. Lambert is a member of the Advisory Board of the National Gallery of Canada, President of the Quebec section of the Canadian Conference of the Arts, and President of the International Confederation of Architectural Museums. As an extension of her interest in the urban environment, she founded the Centre Canadien d'Architecture in Montreal as a museum and study center in 1979.

James Stirling has been a major force in the architectural profession for more than twenty years. The son of a ship engineer, Mr. Stirling was born in Glasgow in 1926 and raised in Liverpool. He received his professional education at the Liverpool University School of Architecture from 1945 to 1950 and formed a partnership with James Gowan in 1955. The first of his significant designs to be built was for the Langham Flats at Ham Common in Richmond.

The acclaimed Leicester University Engineering Building in England, 1959–63, put Mr. Stirling in the forefront of his profession. After his partnership with Mr. Gowan was dissolved in 1963, he went on to design the Cambridge University History Faculty Building, 1964–67, a residential expansion for St. Andrews University in Scotland, 1964–68, and the Olivetti Training School in Haslemere, 1969–72.

In 1971 Mr. Stirling began a partnership with Michael Wilford. Although continuing to design educational facilities such as the expansion of the Rice University School of Architecture in 1979–81, he has since moved into the field of museum architecture, designing the much-acclaimed Staatsgalerie New Building and Workshop Theater in Stuttgart, 1977–84, the Sackler Museum at Harvard University, 1979–84, and the expansion of The Tate Gallery in London, 1985–86. Mr. Stirling has published widely and taught at, among other universities, Cambridge, Yale, and London. He is the recipient of numerous awards, including the Gold Medal of the Royal Institute of British Architects in 1980 and the Pritzker Prize in 1981.

Report of the Jury Chairman
Klaus Herdeg

5.1

5.2.1

5.2.2

5.2.3

194

By unanimous decision, the Jury recommended to the Board of Trustees of The Brooklyn Museum that the entry of architects Arata Isozaki & Associates/James Stewart Polshek and Partners, in a joint venture, be the master plan the Museum should be guided by in its efforts to expand and reorganize the present structure.

In the opinion of most Jury members, the selected scheme is "vastly superior" to the other four entries, if not "in a class by itself." This includes all levels of consideration, from the practical to the symbolic. It was agreed by all jurors that the Isozaki/Polshek master plan will serve the Museum best, for it is most likely to ignite enthusiasm throughout the Brooklyn–New York community as well as nationally and internationally. This momentum is crucial in moving through fund raising into implementation.

The Jury felt that despite its unorthodox appearance—unorthodoxy being the natural consequence of inspired invention—the winning scheme is the one that would most respect the principles of the original turn-of-the-century McKim, Mead & White plan and would, by employing new tactics, give new form to the building and the institution it houses well into the next century.

Of the five entries it is clearly the strongest in both its *internal* strategy for the visitor's orientation and movement through the galleries and other important spaces and its *external* consonance with the monumentality of the McKim, Mead & White fragment and the resurgent civic pride evident in Brooklyn today. The proposal promises to give appropriate form to a world-class museum while, somewhat paradoxically, also showing great sensitivity to the locale into which it is embedded. This kind of sensitivity is expected of any great public building anywhere in the world.

The jurors were impressed by the boldness and originality of the winning scheme, which managed to respect the guiding ideas of McKim, Mead & White's original master plan, an almost acrobatic act. The scheme's invention resides not so much in any particular part, but in the assembly of the

5.1. The Brooklyn Museum, aerial view of north (front) elevation looking southeast, 1986.
5.2. Arata Isozaki & Associates/ James Stewart Polshek and Partners, The Brooklyn Museum Master Plan Competition, competition model, 1986. 1. north elevation; 2. south (Garden) elevation; 3. east elevation.

5.3

5.4.1

5.4.2

5.4.3

5.4.4

5.4.5

parts and above all in a compact new West Wing, which would have three floors of parallel, interconnected galleries tied eastward by a cascade of stairs to a central obelisklike space.

Of all the schemes presented, it alone repossesses McKim, Mead & White's idea of a center crossing from which all areas of the Museum could be reached. On the outside this crossing would be marked by a 150-foot-high obelisk that would give the North Entry mass a more appropriate scale. After climbing the reinstalled Grand Staircase, the visitor would enter the Museum at the reinvigorated third floor, or Piano Nobile, and walk toward this skylit obelisk through a great side-lit, barrel-vaulted hall. For the visitor meandering within the Museum, the obelisk court would become an essential reference point.

While all five schemes reestablish the Piano Nobile and attendant Grand Staircase of the McKim, Mead & White design and respect the commanding axis leading to the southern end of the Cherry Esplanade in both visual and experiential terms, none but the Isozaki/Polshek plan proposes to differentiate so radically, both functionally and experientially, between the left ''lobe,'' as one juror put it, and the right.

To the left, the visitor would find mainly support facilities, such as the Library, the education facilities, and, out on the terrace, the restaurant. With its courtyard paralleling Washington Avenue, the restaurant would not only announce a break with the ''serious'' parts of the Museum but also, by aligning itself with the major Botanic Garden buildings down the street, help to unify further these two great institutions. To be sure there is a proposal for some galleries to ring the Beaux-Arts Court, which is located in the left ''lobe.'' However, most of the galleries, and with them the major collections, are to be found in the right ''lobe,'' with the shops—the only major support facilities—adjoining them. Separating the loading docks for the restaurant and miscellaneous goods from those for art shipment and storage un-

5.3. McKim, Mead & White, The Brooklyn Museum (proposed), plaster model circa 1911, south (Garden) elevation.
5.4. The Brooklyn Museum Master Plan Competition, competition models, south (Garden) elevation, 1986. 1. Atkin, Voith & Associates with Rothzeid Kaiserman Thomson & Bee; 2. Kohn Pedersen Fox; 3. Skidmore, Owings & Merrill with The Vitetta Group/Studio Four; 4. Voorsanger & Mills Associates; 5. Arata Isozaki & Associates/James Stewart Polshek and Partners.

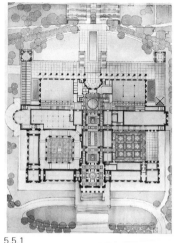

5.5.1

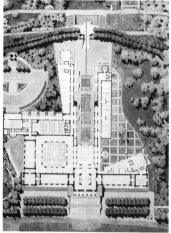

5.5.4

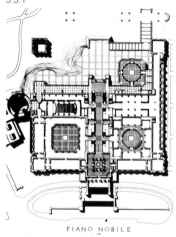

PIANO NOBILE

5.5.2

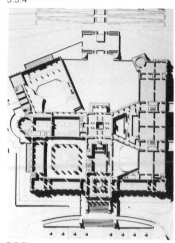

5.5.5

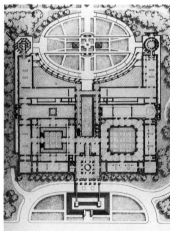

5.5.3

derneath their respective facilities further reinforces this strategy. The fact that all art storage would be above ground was particularly appreciated by the jurors representing the Museum.

In sum, the Jury found extraordinary merit in this new principle of *differentiating* the eastern half of the Museum from the western. None of the other master plans embodies this kind of strategic decision.

Some jurors were initially drawn to the Atkin, Voith & Associates proposal because of its external repose, which would emanate chiefly from its south garden facade. Most jurors felt that this plan's long axially disposed hall would propel the visitor more toward the Garden than into the galleries. Many argued that orientation would be difficult to maintain with most of the galleries located a floor below the Piano Nobile.

Some jurors criticized the proportional quality of the Atkin, Voith gallery wings. A bit awkward individually, as a collection they would not make a coherent whole. Specifically, it seemed that the unified treatment of the southern garden front would jar with the unfinished look of the western front facing Osborne Terrace. In addition, the rearrangement of phasing, almost certain to occur with respect to the availability of financial resources and other demands, was seen as a problem, as it also was in the Kohn Pedersen Fox and Skidmore, Owings & Merrill plans.

Both the Kohn Pedersen Fox and Skidmore, Owings & Merrill presentations were recognized by most jurors as too restrained in massing and external treatment as well as in internal organization. Many jurors found the separate education building along Washington Avenue in the Kohn Pedersen Fox scheme attractive for its appropriate scale, for its relative freedom from the main body of the Museum, and for its interplay with Guider Park. However, the great court leading to the south terrace and the Garden, the Jury felt, would be either a large interior space too much onto itself or a direct conduit to the Garden, virtually bypassing

5.5. The Brooklyn Museum Master Plan Competition, Piano Nobile plan, 1986. 1. Atkin, Voith & Associates with Rothzeid Kaiserman Thomson & Bee; 2. Kohn Pedersen Fox; 3. Skidmore, Owings & Merrill with The Vitetta Group/Studio Four; 4. Voorsanger & Mills Associates; 5. Arata Isozaki & Associates/James Stewart Polshek and Partners.

5.6.2

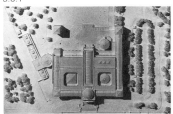

5.6.1

5.6.3

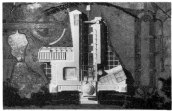

5.6.4

5.6.5

the galleries and the other important spaces of the Museum. Although the Kohn Pedersen Fox scheme is one of three proposals—the others being by Skidmore, Owings & Merrill and Isozaki/Polshek—that develop a full-length new West Wing, the purpose, aesthetically or otherwise, of a 350-foot-long colonnade running a story and a half above Osborne Terrace was obscure. In contrast, the jurors were impressed with the way in which the entire length and height of the winning scheme's west facade (500 × 100 feet) would be given public meaning as a backdrop to an outdoor amphitheater proposed on the eastern slope of Mount Prospect Park. Only in the Isozaki/Polshek proposal was this undeveloped land between the Library on Grand Army Plaza and The Brooklyn Museum taken into consideration, let alone designed as another landscaping feature of public use similar to those parts of the Botanic Garden which in the original McKim, Mead & White plan were meant to have a kind of symbiotic relationship with the Museum.

The Skidmore, Owings & Merrill proposal shares a low-key attitude with those of Atkin, Voith and Kohn Pedersen Fox, but with a difference: this master plan is by far the most formal of the five the Jury examined—not only because of its south colonnade, which would line half an oval terrace of gigantic dimensions (400 × 120 feet), but also because of the manner in which its exterior and interior spaces would be composed. Here, the Jury felt that the Great Court (skewered like the other four schemes' comparable spaces, by the great entry-to-garden axis) would, by being open to the sky, divide the Museum, to a greater extent than the other plans, into two halves of *similar* character. Consequently, problems of orientation would be exacerbated and the visitor's choice of movement lessened rather than amplified by the sequence of spaces. One might expect, looking at the scheme's exterior appearance, a more coherent interior experience. In its relationship to Osborne Terrace and Mount Prospect Park, the Skidmore, Owings & Merrill plan is comparable to the Kohn Pedersen Fox proposal.

197

5.6. The Brooklyn Museum Master Plan Competition, competition models, aerial view, 1986. 1. Atkin, Voith & Associates with Rothzeid Kaiserman Thomson & Bee; 2. Kohn Pedersen Fox; 3. Skidmore, Owings & Merrill with The Vitetta Group/Studio Four; 4. Voorsanger & Mills Associates; 5. Arata Isozaki & Associates/James Stewart Polshek and Partners.

5.7.1

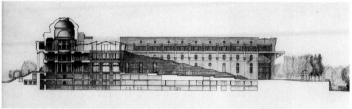

5.7.2

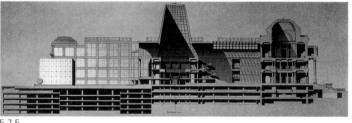

5.7.3

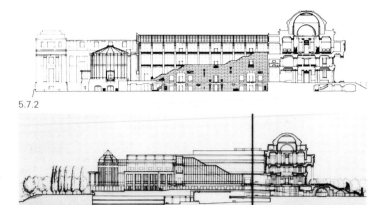

5.7.4

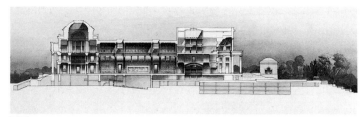

5.7.5

The Jury noted that the master plans of Atkin, Voith; Kohn Pedersen Fox; and Skidmore, Owings & Merrill have certain other common attributes. Each tries to stake out the original territory of the McKim, Mead & White plan rather than adapt, interpret, or exploit its most potent principles as McKim, Mead and White did in 1893 with Durand's museum prototype of 1803.

In these three schemes, the existing fragment is, in effect, built into a new whole governed by new principles such as bilaterally symmetrical rather than centrally organized primary movement through the Museum. The Jury felt that, besides presenting difficulties in absorbing the recently built Wing H, these plans would curtail the visitor's choice of movement—whether in straight sequence, thematic loops, or spot visits that involve shortcuts.

The proposed massing of each of the three schemes is a low profile, perhaps too respectful of the existing North Entry dome, for there would be, in the Jury's judgment, too little distinction between old and new. The Jury felt that, while the motives guiding these decisions are understandable and consistent in most instances, they have the result of producing three schemes unlikely to survive program and phasing changes over the next two or three decades. (For different reasons this was also felt to be true of the Voorsanger & Mills proposal.)

The more or less constant roof height and minimal plastic contrast in the proposals from Atkin, Voith, from Skidmore, Owings & Merrill, and from Kohn Pedersen Fox would make their buildings appear more passive than active, and this, the Jury agreed, is the opposite of what The Brooklyn Museum wants. In considering the proposal of Voorsanger & Mills, at least one Jury member thought it an interesting approach to treat the McKim, Mead & White fragment, which now makes up the entire Museum, as a found object, adding new wings to it in a radically different architectural language. But the jurors also believed the result of this proposal would be a split Museum with a mix of functions on

5.7. The Brooklyn Museum Master Plan Competition, north-south longitudinal section, 1986. 1. Atkin, Voith & Associates with Rothzeid Kaiserman Thomson & Bee; 2. Kohn Pedersen Fox; 3. Skidmore, Owings & Merrill with The Vitetta Group/Studio Four; 4. Voorsanger & Mills Associates; 5. Arata Isozaki & Associates/James Stewart Polshek and Partners.

5.8.1

5.8.2

5.8.3

5.8.4

5.8.5

either side. The choice of movement through the galleries would be very limited, if not leading the visitor to virtual dead ends, and the galleries themselves would be difficult to adjust in size and sequence.

Like the Skidmore, Owings & Merrill proposal, the Voorsanger & Mills plan proposes an open court leading from the North Entry toward the Cherry Esplanade, but unlike any other scheme the court would become another garden. By placing the restaurant on the fourth floor of the longer of the two main gallery wings, this scheme would be the only one to exploit the breathtaking views to be enjoyed of the Verrazzano Bridge to the south and lower Manhattan to the west. It is an important detail of this scheme that the jurors appreciated.

Finally, addressing all five entries, the Jury would like to commend all the competitors for their high level of performance in content and presentation. The collective work merits a public exhibition and an even wider audience through publication in this book.

Conclusions

Because this competition was intended to produce a master plan encompassing perhaps twenty years or more as opposed to a scheme covering a much shorter time span, it is important to recall some primary distinctions between the two. The first is presumably a plan of action based on firm principles, leaving room for some change. For instance, The Brooklyn Museum must expect certain program and phasing changes, dictated perhaps by the pace of its fund raising, the expansion of collections, or changes in curatorial policy. The second type of plan is usually much simpler, depending on the building's size and available funds, and is adopted with the attitude, "We like it, we build it."

For these reasons, The Brooklyn Museum Jury went in search of the proposal with the most organizational and plastic strength—the master plan that would not become a straight jacket as demands change over the many years it

5.8. The Brooklyn Museum Master Plan Competition, competition models, aerial view of proposed West Wing, 1986.
1. Atkin, Voith & Associates with Rothzeid Kaiserman Thomson & Bee; 2. Kohn Pedersen Fox; 3. Skidmore, Owings & Merrill with The Vitetta Group/Studio Four; 4. Voorsanger & Mills Associates; 5. Arata Isozaki & Associates/James Stewart Polshek and Partners.

will take to raise the funds and build the building. In this respect, the jurors felt, the winning entry excelled.

Two, perhaps obvious, equations were drawn by the Jury. First, the faster the funds are raised, the greater the likelihood of implementation of the entire plan. Second, if early on a substantial portion of the new construction, say the all-important new West Wing, is built, it will be that much more clear to the public, the media, and potential donors that The Brooklyn Museum means business. The desire to fill in this "frame" would in all likelihood be irresistible, thus keeping the momentum going.

The Jury itself was remarkable in that *all* seven jurors, three "experts" and four "laymen," participated with equal enthusiasm in the discussions that culminated in our unanimous decision. This was made possible by meticulous preparations that allowed the Jury to enter the judging room ready to see and compare.

Now having completed the process, all jurors emphatically agree that not only was the Master Plan Competition worth the effort but by its very success recommends itself. In the words of one of the jurors from the Museum's Board of Trustees, "The education that I personally have received during the last six months, particularly through the last three days, is going to make myself and the Museum more enlightened clients. . . . Architect and client will have a much better chance to realize these plans. . . . The process itself has given the architect and the client a head start on understanding each other."

Appendixes

Appendix A: Competition Personnel

Staff

Project Director: Joan Darragh, Vice Director for Planning, The Brooklyn Museum

Competition Advisor: Terrance R. Williams, FAIA, Williams + Garretson

Competition Program Coordinator: Kevin Perry, Williams + Garretson

Assistant to the Jury Chairman: Gwendolyn Herr Glass, AIA, The Brooklyn Museum

Publication and Exhibition Coordination: Bailey Van Hook, The Brooklyn Museum

Manuscript Production: Wanda Sweat, The Brooklyn Museum

Committees

Selection Committee

Alastair B. Martin, Chairman, Board of Trustees, The Brooklyn Museum

Robert S. Rubin, President, Board of Trustees, The Brooklyn Museum

John A. Friede, Trustee, Chairman, Plan and Scope Committee, The Brooklyn Museum

Jeffrey C. Keil, Trustee, Chairman, Building Committee, The Brooklyn Museum

Mrs. Carl Selden, Trustee, The Brooklyn Museum

Linda Adams, Cultural Liaison, Office of the Brooklyn Borough President

Thomas Mangan, Director of Facilities, Department of Cultural Affairs, the Mayor's Office, New York City

Ronay Menschel, Chairperson, Mayor's Advisory Commission for Cultural Affairs, the Mayor's Office, New York City

Robert T. Buck, Director, The Brooklyn Museum

Linda S. Ferber, Chief Curator, The Brooklyn Museum

Reyner Banham, Architectural Critic and Advisor, University of California, Santa Cruz

Joan Darragh, Vice Director for Planning, The Brooklyn Museum (nonvoting)

Terrance R. Williams, FAIA, Competition Advisor (nonvoting)

Technical Review Panel

Joan Darragh, Vice Director for Planning, The Brooklyn Museum

Linda S. Ferber, Chief Curator, The Brooklyn Museum

Daniel Weidmann, Vice Director for Operations, The Brooklyn Museum

Martin Goldman, Goldman, Sokolow & Copeland

Kongal Guellec, Schal Associates, New York

Frank Sanchis, Vice President for Stewardship of Historic Properties, National Trust for Historic Preservation

Peter Casler, Director of Capital Planning and Construction, Brooklyn Botanic Garden

Thomas Mangan, Director of Facilities, Department of Cultural Affairs, The Mayor's Office, New York City

Bruce McDonell, Section Chief, Libraries and Cultural Affairs, Department of General Services, New York City

Terrance R. Williams, Professional Advisor, Williams + Garretson

Kevin Perry, Building Program Coordinator, Williams + Garretson

Jury

Klaus Herdeg (Jury Chairman), Professor of Architecture, Columbia University

Alastair B. Martin, Chairman, Board of Trustees, The Brooklyn Museum

Robert S. Rubin, President, Board of Trustees, The Brooklyn Museum

Jeffrey C. Keil, Trustee, Chairman, Building Committee, The Brooklyn Museum

Robert T. Buck, Director, The Brooklyn Museum

Phyllis Lambert, Architect, President, Centre Canadien d'Architecture, Montreal

James Stirling, Architect, James Stirling Michael Wilford and Associates, London

Competitors

Semifinalists

Atkin, Voith & Associates, Philadelphia

Bower Lewis Thrower/Architects, Philadelphia

Centerbrook with Charles Moore, Essex, Connecticut

Michael Graves, Architects, Princeton, New Jersey

Hammond Beeby and Babka, Inc., Chicago

Hardy Holzman Pfeiffer Associates, New York

Arata Isozaki & Associates/James Stewart Polshek and Partners, Tokyo and New York

Kohn Pedersen Fox, New York

Skidmore, Owings & Merrill, New York

Voorsanger & Mills Associates, New York

Finalists

Atkin, Voith & Associates with Rothzeid Kaiserman Thomson & Bee

Arata Isozaki & Associates/James Stewart Polshek and Partners

Kohn Pedersen Fox

Skidmore, Owings & Merrill with The Vitetta Group/ Studio Four

Voorsanger & Mills Associates

Award of the Jury

Arata Isozaki & Associates/James Stewart Polshek and Partners

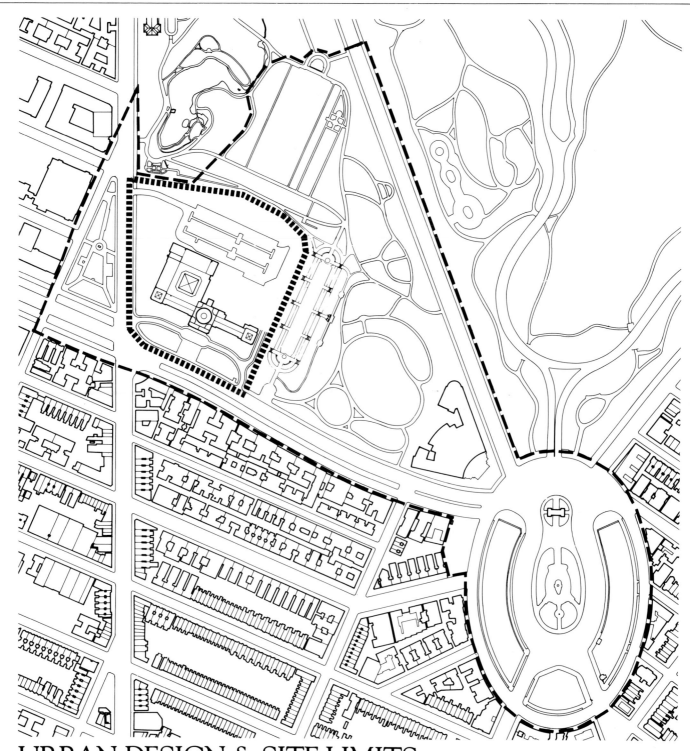

URBAN DESIGN & SITE LIMITS

▪▪▪▪▪▪▪▪▪▪▪▪▪ THE BROOKLYN MUSEUM PROPERTY LINE

— — — — — URBAN DESIGN STUDY LIMITS

THE BROOKLYN MUSEUM MASTER PLAN COMPETITION

Appendix B: Design Guidelines and Program Summary*

Terrance R. Williams

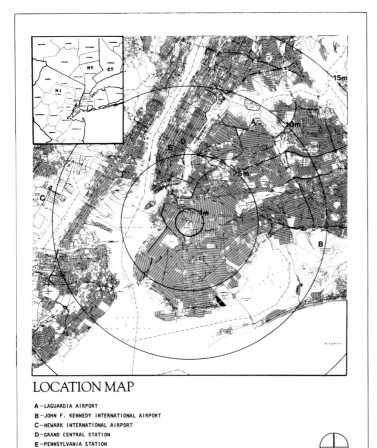

LOCATION MAP

A — LAGUARDIA AIRPORT
B — JOHN F. KENNEDY INTERNATIONAL AIRPORT
C — NEWARK INTERNATIONAL AIRPORT
D — GRAND CENTRAL STATION
E — PENNSYLVANIA STATION

THE BROOKLYN MUSEUM MASTER PLAN COMPETITION

Introduction

The Board of Trustees of The Brooklyn Museum has elected to sponsor an international, single-stage, invitational competition to produce a master plan that will guide the Museum's reorganization and growth into the next century. The key goals are:

• The reorganization and expansion of the facilities for the proper display, study, and care of the collections.
• Expanded educational and special programming facilities.
• The preservation and restoration of the existing landmark building and the design and construction of new facilities in a manner appropriate to and respectful of the Beaux-Arts vocabulary of McKim, Mead & White.
• The integration of the grounds of the Museum and Botanic Garden to increase the benefits of the symbiotic relationship between the institutions.
• The development of a phasing and budgeting strategy so that the master plan can be implemented in stages commensurate with funding and the continued operation of the Museum.

Design Guidelines

Urban Design Considerations. Centrally located in the Borough of Brooklyn, The Brooklyn Museum is the centerpiece of a great urban composition. It includes Prospect Park and Zoo, the Brooklyn Botanic Garden, the Brooklyn Public Library, Mount Prospect Park, Guider Park, Eastern Parkway, and Grand Army Plaza. While it is beyond the scope of this competition to supply all the missing links, the Museum requests that the competitors include in their investigations the integration of all or part of Mount Prospect Park and Guider Park with the Eastern Parkway corridor from Grand Army Plaza to the Parkway entrances of the Museum and the Botanic Garden.

This excerpt was taken from "The Brooklyn Museum Master Plan Competition," January 25, 1986, unpublished manuscript, 120 pp., which was distributed to the competitors.

207

While the Museum is most interested in receiving urban design strategies for the prescribed area, the development of the Museum's master plan can in no way be contingent upon these off-site improvements. All Museum Building Program space must be confined to Museum property. The Museum is committed, however, to doing its share in establishing a design direction for the area that will be of mutual benefit to, and can receive support from, all affected institutions. The single most important urban design consideration, however, is the integration of the Museum and the Botanic Garden.

Predetermined Design Decisions
1. Principal Entry
The principal entry to the Museum is to be restored to its original location under the Rotunda on the third-floor Piano Nobile. The original Piano Nobile entry hall shall be re-created. The selection of interior vocabulary, whether a historical reconstruction or contemporary interpretation, is at the discretion of the architect.

2. Fifth-Floor Rotunda
The fifth-floor Rotunda shall be redesigned using such vocabulary as is appropriate to restore to it the grandeur intended by the McKim, Mead & White design.

3. Third-Floor Court
The skylight court of Wing G cutting between the third and fourth floors shall be historically restored.

4. First-Floor Court
The court of the first and second floors, Wing G, shall be historically restored.

5. Original Galleries
The spaces originally designed as gallery space by McKim, Mead & White are to be returned to their original purpose to the extent that this is possible.

Budget and Phasing. The competitors are to regard incremental construction and phasing of their proposed master plan as a key concern of the Museum. The ability to fund the renovation and additions makes phased implementation imperative. The construction costs of each phase are not to exceed $20 million. Each phase should further the coherence of the Museum and Botanic Garden complex as well as enable the Museum to fulfill all its institutional functions.

Program Summary
A primary consideration for the Museum has been the need for reorganization and expansion. The existing building plant is inadequate in almost all aspects. Gallery space is too limited for the collections, the designated space for special exhibitions is almost nonexistent, and inadequate storage facilities are inappropriate for the proper care and preservation of the works of art. The competitors are asked to reconsider the organization of the entire building in addition to methods of expansion. It is fully expected that almost the entire interior of the building will be rebuilt.

Another key goal of the master plan is to develop an architectural vocabulary that is respectful of the tradition and quality of the original building.

Besides the renovation of the interiors, the Museum wishes to achieve an integration with the Botanic Garden as sensitive as the link projected by the original master plan. The proposals for an addition and new Museum grounds are expected to combine building and Botanic Garden to create a seamless cultural amenity, yet one that satisfies both the aesthetic and security needs of the separate institutions.

Program
All areas are designated in net square feet and include existing as well as proposed footage.
1. Public Entry 17,560
The general public must be able to enter from both Eastern Parkway and the rear.
The school-group entry must be visually and acoustically separated from the general-public entry and act as a holding area for groups.

The Museum requires regular extended-hour entry for the Auditorium, education-program spaces, and the restaurant.

2. Education Program Spaces 45,080

This set of spaces offers educational programs for the general public. While the spaces are expected to form a coherent "campus" within the building, the ability of visitors to interact with the public gallery spaces is crucial for all the educational programs.

3. Retail Shops 10,300

4. Galleries 272,338

A primary design concern for each of the individual collections is to provide a coherent set of galleries that corresponds to the logical organization of the collection. A secondary design goal should be to present the collections to the visitor so that their universal scope can be appreciated. The public path through the Museum should be structured after cultural and geographical patterns.

The Museum's permanent collections break down into four distinct but interrelated cultural units:

- *Western: American Painting and Sculpture; European and Early Modern Painting and Sculpture; Decorative Arts; Costumes and Textiles; Prints and Drawings*
- *Oriental and Islamic*
- *Egyptian, Classical, and Ancient Middle Eastern*
- *African, Oceanic, and New World*

In addition to the permanent collections, special-exhibition galleries are an essential part of the Museum's program. Special exhibitions are the main means of attracting the public to the Museum, making the location of these galleries particularly important. The special-exhibition galleries should encourage public circulation through the Museum.

5. Food Services 15,650

Food Services will operate three facilities and provide catering for selected locations within the Museum. The Museum Cafeteria will service the general public. The Museum Restaurant will offer table service and will be divided into three or four dining rooms with the ability to accommodate private parties. The Employee Cafeteria will service the Museum staff for both served meals and brown-bag lunches.

6. Library and Research 24,420

The Library consists of two major research collections—the Art Reference Library and the Wilbour Library of Egyptology.

7. Offices: Administration and Curatorial 64,870

8. Collection Management: Art Storage, Conservation, and Registration 128,420

Art Storage Facilities must be flexible and large enough to accommodate the collections designated for each area. The expansion of storage facilities must be planned for in the phasing of the building. Art storage must not be located in the basement and must be planned for areas of the building free of all potentially damaging systems and elements.

9. Mechanical 50,000

10. Operations 44,750

11. Museum Grounds and Parking

The Museum grounds are to be integrated with those of the Botanic Garden. The Museum parking is to be placed in a built garage.

Competitors are encouraged to use the rear security-controlled grounds for display of the outstanding architectural fragment collection and freestanding sculpture, and for small performances.

Appendix C: Chronology of The Brooklyn Museum
Compiled by Deirdre E. Lawrence

1823 A group of concerned citizens of the Village of Brooklyn organizes the Brooklyn Apprentices' Library Association.

1825 Plans are made for a library building. On July 4, General Lafayette, on a triumphal tour of America, lays the cornerstone for the new building in Brooklyn Heights.

1841 Library moves to quarters in the Lyceum Building on Washington Street, housing collections previously reported by acting librarian Walt Whitman to have reached 1,200 volumes.

1843 The Apprentices' Library and the Brooklyn Lyceum are legally consolidated and renamed The Brooklyn Institute.

1846 Institute announces plans for a permanent gallery of fine arts.

1851 Augustus Graham, one of the original founders of the Apprentices' Library, dies and leaves a major bequest to the Institute for the acquisition of books, natural-history specimens, and paintings by American artists, as well as for support of free lectures and a school of design.

1867 Washington Street building of The Brooklyn Institute undergoes major renovation to accommodate growing collections as well as educational activities.

1888 An Institute committee plans for a new Museum building that would be a unique institution combining the arts and sciences. Legislation is passed to set aside land adjacent to Prospect Park for art and educational institutions.

1890 The Institute is reorganized into The Brooklyn Institute of Arts and Sciences, with departments ranging from anthropology to zoology. The new Institute eventually becomes the parent of the Brooklyn Academy of Music, the Brooklyn Botanic Garden, and the

Brooklyn Children's Museum, as well as The Brooklyn Museum.

Fire damages the Institute building, and the collections are stored in nearby institutions.

1893 The Institute's Department of Architecture organizes an architectural competition to provide a design for a Museum building. The firm of McKim, Mead & White is selected.

1895 Brooklyn Mayor Charles Schieren lays the cornerstone for the Museum building.

1897 The West Wing is completed, the collections are installed, and the building is opened to the public.

1899 The collections are organized within three departments: Fine Arts, Natural Sciences, and Ethnology.

The first Children's Museum in the world is established as a branch of The Brooklyn Institute of Arts and Sciences.

1905 Institute Board of Directors sets up acquisition fund to encourage contributions from the membership.

1906 The Museum begins excavations in Egypt, which continue to present day in the Precinct of Mut at South Karnak.

1907 The East Wing and the Central Pavilion with its Grand Staircase are completed.

The art collection is composed of 532 paintings, watercolors, and photographs as well as plaster casts and decorative arts. Great quantities of archaeological, ethnographic, and natural-history material are accumulated through Museum expeditions.

1915 Colonel Robert Woodward, an Institute Trustee for twenty-five years, leaves the Museum his private art collection as well as funds for its endowment.

1916 Major international exhibition program is begun with the *Exhibition of Contemporary Swedish Art*.

The heirs of Charles Edwin Wilbour, a pioneer American Egyptologist, donate his collection of art objects and his library to the Museum. These items from Wilbour's collection become the cornerstone of the Museum's world-renowned Egyptian collection and are later augmented by an endowment fund given in Wilbour's honor by his son.

William H. Fox, the Institute's Director of Museums from 1914 to 1933, shortens the title of the Central Museum of The Brooklyn Institute of Arts and Sciences to The Brooklyn Museum.

1920 A subway stop is opened in front of the Museum, and attendance increases markedly.

1922 Augustus Healy, President of The Brooklyn Institute for twenty-five years, leaves the Museum his personal collection of paintings and other works of art as well as endowment funds.

1923 The Museum holds a precedent-setting exhibition that interprets objects from its African collection as fine art rather than ethnographic specimens.

1926 The Museum organizes the *International Exhibition of Modern Art*, one of the largest and most comprehensive showings of modern art yet held in America.

1927 Last two sections of the Museum completed according to the original McKim, Mead & White plans.

1929 The Museum opens twenty-one American period rooms; in time there are twenty-eight rooms ranging in date from 1675 to 1928.

1934 Museum establishes a new collecting policy emphasizing the fine arts, cultural history, and the social and industrial aspects of art. The natural-history collections are discontinued and dispersed to several institutions, including the Brooklyn Children's Museum, the Brooklyn Botanic Garden, and the American Museum of Natural History.

The front stairs are removed and a new entry hall created.

1935 The collections are rearranged in chronological order, beginning with the prehistoric period on the main floor and continuing up to the Gallery of Living Artists on the top floor.

1941 The Brooklyn Museum Art School, jointly organized by The Brooklyn Institute and the Brooklyn Art Association in 1891 and previously housed in the Brooklyn Academy of Music, is installed in the Museum.

1948 The Brooklyn Museum purchases the Egyptian holdings of the New-York Historical Society.

The Edward C. Blum Design Laboratory is opened to encourage the study of design. In the 1960s the Laboratory is transferred to the Fashion Institute of Technology.

1950 Plans for major renovation of the entire Museum are begun by the architectural firm of Brown, Lawford and Forbes.

1953 The Museum becomes the first American art museum to open a series of nineteenth-century period rooms.

1964 Daniel Chester French's allegorical figures of Brooklyn and Manhattan are removed from the Manhattan Bridge and placed on either side of the Museum's main entrance.

212 **1966** The Frieda Schiff Warburg Memorial Sculpture

Garden, containing architectural fragments from demolished New York buildings, is opened in the rear of the Museum.

The Brooklyn Museum is designated a landmark by the New York City Landmarks Preservation Commission.

1970 The Brooklyn Academy of Music becomes the first of the departments comprising The Brooklyn Institute of Arts and Sciences to be reorganized as an independent institution.

1976 The New York City Landmarks Commission approves the addition to the rear of the Museum of a new service extension designed by Prentice & Chan, Ohlhausen.

1977 A ground-breaking ceremony is held for the new extension.

The Brooklyn Museum is added to the National Register of Historic Places.

1985 The Art School is closed and the adult classes are transferred to Pratt Institute to join that institution's long-established fine arts program.

1986 The Master Plan Competition Jury selects Arata Isozaki & Associates/James Stewart Polshek and Partners to devise a new master plan to improve existing conditions and provide for the Museum's growth into the next century.

Photograph Credits

All photographs are from the collection of The Brooklyn Museum except where noted in the captions. Where the photographers are known, they are acknowledged here:

Shigeo Anzai: photograph of Arata Isozaki
Patricia Layman Bazelon: pages 4–5, Intro.2, 2.15, 2.20, 2.27, 2.28, 2.29, 2.30. 2.31, photograph of Robert T. Buck
Tom Bernard: Intro.5
© Richard Bryant: Intro.4
Martin Charles: Intro.1
Robert Day: photograph of James Stewart Polshek
Detroit Photographing and Publishing Company: 1.2
Richard Dooner: 2.9
© Nathaniel Lieberman: 1.18, 4.1, 4.13, 4.23, 4.35, 4.46, 5.2.1, 5.2.3, 5.3, 5.4.1–5, 5.6.1–5, 5.8.1, 5.8.3–5.
Jock Pottle: 5.8.2
Skyviews: page 6, 2.26, 5.1
Ralph Steiner: 2.4
© Ezra Stoller/ESTO: Intro.3